D0850215

THE LOYALIST AMERICANS
A Focus on Greater New York

THE LOYALIST AMERICANS
A Focus
on Greater New York

*Edited by Robert A. East
and Jacob Judd*

SLEEPY HOLLOW RESTORATIONS

TARRYTOWN, NEW YORK

Library of Congress Cataloging in Publication Data
Main entry under title:
The Loyalist Americans.
Essays presented at a conference held at Tarrytown, N. Y., Nov. 2-3, 1973,
and sponsored by Sleepy Hollow Restorations and
the New York State American Revolution Bicentennial Commission.
Bibliography: p.
Includes index.
1. American loyalists—New York (State)—Congresses.
2. New York (State)—Politics and government—Revolution,
    1775-1783—Congresses.
I. East, Robert Abraham, 1909-
II. Judd, Jacob, 1929-
III. Sleepy Hollow Restorations, Tarrytown, N.Y.
IV. New York State American Revolution Bicentennial Commission.
F123.L7   973.3'14   74-7846
ISBN 0-912882-14-X

For information, address the publisher:
Sleepy Hollow Restorations, Inc.
Tarrytown, New York 10591

ISBN 0-912882-14-X
Library of Congress Catalog Card Number: 74-7846

First Printing

Printed in The United States of America
Designed by Ray Freiman

CONTENTS

ILLUSTRATIONS

James Rivington

James Rivington was a well-known Loyalist printer and the editor of *Rivington's New-York Gazeteer*, published in New York City. This woodcut, [on page ix, also used on the jacket of this book] depicting him "hanging by his neck in effigy by the townspeople of New Brunswick," was published in his newspaper April 20, 1775. (Courtesy The New-York Historical Society)

O VER SIXTY YEARS AGO the sentiment was voiced that the time was thankfully past when it was necessary to speak "with bated breath" on behalf of the American Loyalists; yet only recently a writer has lamented that the story of the Loyalists in the American Revolution has yet to be integrated into our history.* An interval of over half a century between these two statements illustrates our persistent unwillingness to recognize a painful aspect of our early national development. Only with the approach of the Bicentennial celebration of the American Revolution are we carefully reassessing the Loyalist situation, and accepting the fact that there were some Americans, in those stirring times, who disagreed with the revolutionary fervor.

A great deal of sentiment for Crown allegiance continued to exist in the Middle Colonies, well beyond the time when the Declaration of Independence was generally accepted elsewhere. What made so many New Yorkers and Jerseyites so anti-revolutionary is still a subject for controversy and debate. It is our objective in these studies to help clarify the issues confronting the citizenry of the Middle Colonies, and especially those who lived in the fertile valley of the Hudson River. No doubt it should be borne in mind that the Middle Colonies

---

* H.E. Egerton, ed., *The Royal Commission on the Losses and Services of American Loyalists*, 1783–1785 (Arno Press reprint, New York, 1969) p. xiii; Alden T. Vaughan and George A. Billias, eds., *Perspectives on Early American History* (New York, 1973), p. 284.

had become the breadbasket of the British-American empire, and had developed a tremendous stake in the intercolonial and overseas trade under the protection of the royal fleet. The two major seaports of Philadelphia and New York were thriving, bustling communities in pre-1776 days. Was all this to be cast aside?

The colonies of New York and New Jersey had flourished in many ways under British control. Although originally founded and settled by the Dutch, they did not really move ahead until 1664 when they became part of the proprietorship of James, Duke of York, heir apparent to the English throne. When James was made King, they had become royal colonies. While other royal provinces, particularly Massachusetts and Virginia, frequently complained about restraints imposed on them by the Trade and Navigation Acts, the Middle Colonies had prospered from the first. English rule had been benevolent and good. Must this all come to naught?

In the recent past, some writers may have overemphasized the degree of allegiance paid to the King by the American colonists (thus overemphasizing the wrenching effect which the revolutionary movement was to have), but in any case a philosophy of self-interestedness had surely grown up in the century and a half of American dependency. Those who had fared well as part of the "establishment" were now suddenly confronted with a situation in which they stood to lose everything. What choice would they make?

The most difficult problem confronting the Americans of our Revolutionary Era involved matters of principle. What are the fundamental rights of man? Did not the so-called English "Constitution" recognize and protect life, liberty, and property? Could such rights be violated in the English colonies? Should bonds of political union therefore be sundered? Could one person be totally "right," and his opposite totally "wrong"?

Each person living at the time of the American Revolution was confronted with such questions. Each had to make a decision based on his or her own conscience, and take the consequences.

xii

This collection of original essays is based upon papers presented at a conference on The Loyalist Americans sponsored by Sleepy Hollow Restorations and the New York State American Revolution Bicentennial Commission at Tarrytown, New York, November 2 and 3, 1973. Jacob Judd's paper was especially prepared for this edition. Robert A. East served as Chairman of the conference and Jacob Judd oversaw the entire program. Its focus upon the American Loyalists is not only upon the "whys and wherefores" but upon the "therefores." Decisions about allegiance were to be followed by problems of war.

Professor Catherine Crary, who died shortly after the conference, had not only prepared her paper with her customary meticulous scholarship but also delivered it in person with her customary dynamism. Those present will always remember her stimulating presentation and her courageous spirit.

The editors wish to thank Professor Glenn Weaver of Trinity College; Dr. James E. Mooney, Assistant Director of The Historical Society of Pennsylvania; and Professor Marcus Cunliffe of The University of Sussex, Visiting Professor of History at The University of Michigan, for their conference comments, which aided in the preparation of this volume.

History is the study of individuals and of their actions. It is the intent of these essays to cast additional light on how some Americans reacted to an awesome question.

ROBERT A. EAST
Executive Director
Program for Loyalist Studies and Publications
Graduate Center City University of New York

JACOB JUDD
Herbert H. Lehman College
City University of New York

"A Topographical Map of Hudson's River," (page 2) drawn by
Claude Joseph Sauthier and engraved by William Faden in
London in 1776. (Courtesy The British Museum)

THE LOYALIST AMERICANS
A Focus on Greater New York

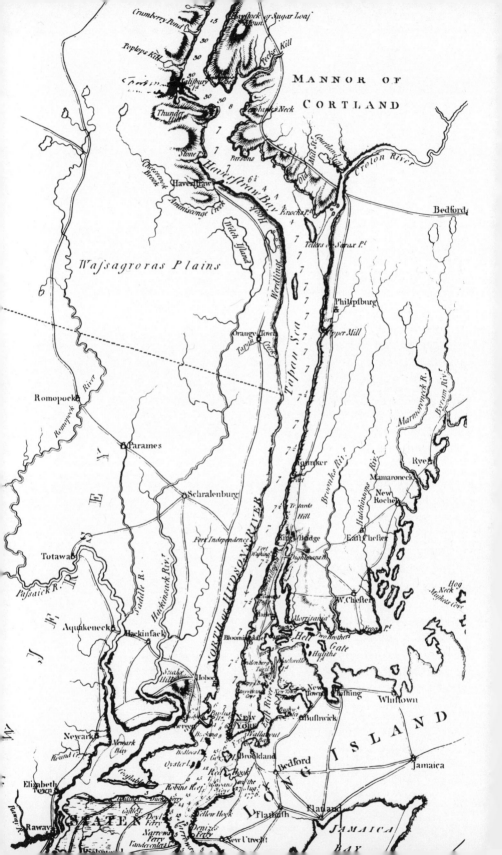

The Loyalist Problem In The Lower Hudson Valley: The British Perspective

John Shy

THE AMERICAN REVOLUTION was a civil war. Not until the twentieth century did historians, with a very few notable exceptions, find that fact interesting; and only in the last decade or so have historians begun to find it very interesting. The best estimate is that between a fifth and a quarter of the white population—perhaps a half million people—behaved in ways that enable us to identify them as Loyalist; and we cannot help but wonder what such a large, actively dissenting minority means for our understanding of the nature of the Revolution.[1]

Certain specific questions keep coming to the surface as we ponder the significance of Loyalism. One—which Paul Smith, William Willcox, and Piers Mackesy have recently done much to answer—concerns apparent British inability to tap effectively this large reservoir of political sentiment and military potential.[2] Could the British government and high command, given an earlier, clearer sense of the kind of war they were involved in, have used militant Loyalism to build a basis for ultimate pacification of a weary, bankrupt rebel movement?

A second question, less frequently raised but always lurking beneath the surface of every comparative discussion of the American Revolution, concerns violence: The American Revolution somehow avoided the extremes of murderous behavior that so disfigured and poisoned other great revolutions, or did it? Hannah Arendt has brilliantly contrasted the limited, almost benign, and therefore successful quality of the American Revolution, with the untidy, horrific failure of the French

3

Revolution to achieve a just and stable society.[3] But Robert Palmer, in an undeveloped few paragraphs in his *Age of the Democratic Revolution*, suggests that, measured by the relative numbers of refugees from revolution, the American may have been as violently intolerant as the French; and in a short article Gordon Wood, drawing on the most recent studies of European mobs in the eighteenth century, also concludes that the alleged differences between the amount and quality of violence in Europe and America may be less important than the similarities.[4] With thousands of armed Loyalists in the field, the tentative thoughts of Palmer and Wood indeed seem plausible.

The third question grows directly out of the second: If Palmer and Wood are right, and the civil, internecine violence of the American Revolution was not so very different from what the histories of other civil wars and revolutions would lead us to expect, then how do we explain the relatively quick subsidence of the Tory issue after the war? Palmer suggests that, unlike France, the American counterrevolutionary refugees never returned, creating an illusion of tranquility and unity in the postwar Republic. But only a fraction of the half-million Loyalists were ever able or perhaps willing to emigrate, and my own impression is that more returned than Palmer thinks. Most Loyalists appear to have been reintegrated, speedily and painlessly, into American society, and Hannah Arendt's conclusion, if not her explanation, seems supported by that fact— if it is a fact.[5] There was no Red Terror of 1783, not even in Bergen and Westchester Counties, or in Ninety-Six District of South Carolina, to match the Terrors, both Red and White, described for France so graphically by Richard Cobb.[6] These are very hard questions, which beg for further inquiry and yet resist straightforward research, about the nature of the American Revolution. Perhaps we can begin by pulling them down from the plane of abstraction and comparison onto a level where the scale is human, where people have names and personalities, events the concreteness and complexity of real life, and ultimate consequences are as hazy as the future itself.

In the latter half of 1776, British forces occupied Staten Island and drove the rebels out of western Long Island and off Manhattan. For the next six years the military situation changed very little. Based solidly on the three great islands that form New York harbor, the British made their military presence felt throughout Long Island, west and north into New Jersey as far as the Watchung and Ramapo Mountains, into Westchester County to the Croton River, and even into the western part of Fairfield County, Connecticut. Never, of course, could the British control or dominate this vast arc of territory, but they did create conditions under which rebellion did not flourish. Unlike those in the hinterlands of New England, Pennsylvania, and Virginia, armed American rebels around New York City were unable to intimidate their recalcitrant or apathetic neighbors. Instead, repeated British forays broke up rebel committees, killed, captured, and dispersed their leaders, and encouraged the reluctant and the timid to stand up for their king.

Within a year after the seizure of New York, British strategy began to undergo a reappraisal that was truly agonizing. A small field army under Burgoyne had just been lost at Saratoga, the French were moving toward open intervention, and little had been accomplished by the Howe brothers' elaborate invasion of Pennsylvania. Rebellion was still intact, and thus far the costly efforts made to put it down seemed futile. A new approach was needed. The new approach which emerged during 1778 emphasized the role of loyal Americans. It was at last admitted that, ultimately, restored British authority would have to depend on Americans themselves, and that even the strongest army and navy could do no more than create favorable conditions for the Americanization of the war. Moreover, facing a global war against France, the British government and high command found it convenient to draw more heavily upon American military manpower, and to justify a long, expensive war to an unhappy public on the ground that the king had a solemn commitment to defend his numerous American supporters against rebel vengeance. Thus, during 1778, Loyalists moved from the periphery toward the center of the war. As they did so, the lower Hudson Valley became especially important as the place where first-hand British impressions of American Loyalism were most readily and influentially formed.

Months before the British army and navy arrived in 1776, the whole area had become notorious for its political apathy and open opposition to the Revolution. The Westchester committee formed to enforce the boycott of trade with Britain had petitioned the New York Provincial Congress for an armed guard to protect its meetings against Tory assault.[7] In Bergen County, across the Hudson, an open election had returned a distinctly counterrevolutionary delegation to the New Jersey Provincial Congress.[8] Orange County south of the Highlands (modern Rockland County) had much the same kind of experience. Many local explanations have been advanced for the strength of Loyalism in the lower Hudson Valley—Anglo-Dutch antagonism, splits within the Dutch Reformed Church, hatred of the great landlords—but none that can account for the entire region. In any case, the British in 1776 moved their main base into an unusually favorable political environment. Oliver DeLancey and Beverley Robinson in New York, Cortlandt Skinner in New Jersey, and several other leading Loyalists recruited thousands of American soldiers to fight for the king in provincial battalions. Well before the agonizing reappraisal of strategy in 1778, British commanders were seeing a good deal of Loyalism in action.

What, actually, did they see? They saw, it seems, what they wanted to see. Two very different views of the significance of Loyalism were emerging by 1778. For some, like the young Earl of Carlisle, who headed the peace commission sent to America by the North government, no hopes should be placed in widespread American loyalty:

The leaders . . . are too powerful; the common people hate us in their hearts, notwithstanding all that is said of their secret attachment to the mother country. . . . Formerly, when things were better for us, there was an appearance of friendship by their coming in for pardons, that might have deceived even those who have been most acquainted with them. But no sooner our situation was the least altered for the worse, but these friends were the first to fire upon us. . . . In our present condition the only friends we have, or are likely to have, are those who are absolutely ruined for us. . . . [9]

Carlisle and his fellow peace commissioners favored a strategy of destruction—"a war of expedition" as it was called—laying waste American towns, forcing every colonial to choose one side or the other. If terrorism became the new strategy, no one was readier to carry it out than armed Loyalists. Major Patrick Ferguson, who would die two years later at King's Mountain (North Carolina) at the head of armed Loyalists, agreed with Carlisle: "It is surely become necessary," he wrote to General Clinton, "to exert a degree of severity, which would not have been justifyable at the beginning. . . . if necessary lay waste the Country." Ferguson wanted to promise every Loyalist recruit a farm, which would "at once detach from the Rebels, the common Irish and other Europeans who make the Strength of their armys."[10]

For others, equally able to observe, the evidence of American Loyalism conveyed a different message. Peter DuBois, an active New Jersey Loyalist, a spy for the British, and later a police magistrate in occupied New York City, argued that visible Loyalism was only the tip of an iceberg. "General discontent prevails," he wrote to Clinton, "amongst the most disloyal and disaffected." In Bergen County not more than two hundred people supported the rebellion, and even those were scattered—at Closter near the Hudson, at Paramus in the center of the county and westward around Preakness, and "some pestilent fellows" up in the hills around Ringwood.[11] A flow of intelligence reports into Clinton's headquarters told the same story, of rebel weakness and demoralization; these reports were confirmed by a stream of deserters from the Continental Army, and even by the behavior of some captured rebel officers, who appear to have turned completely against the Revolution. Captain Moore Fauntleroy of Moylan's 4th Continental Dragoons, captured at Germantown and a member of one of the First Families of Virginia, told the British commissary of prisoners that "our affairs are as dark as they can be; & I really believe the game is up." He promised to send back intelligence reports while on parole, and he did. After going home to Virginia and returning to New York, Captain Fauntleroy said that "the whole continent is starving. . . . The Continental money is not worth a curse . . . everybody is tired; & those red-hot Virginians who were so violent are all crying out for Peace; & I don't wonder at it, for by God that Province at least will be starved."[12] Other reports supported Fauntleroy: "There is a Number of persons in this Neighbourhood," said one from Bedford in Westchester, "who have been the first Leading Men that are almost ripe to join you"; and in fact James Holmes of Bedford, who had commanded a rebel battalion of Westchester militia until 1777, was just then changing sides, and would end the war leading a force of Westchester Loyalist refugees.[13]

The picture of Loyalism in the area around New York, then, was not altogether clear. Still less clear was what to do about it. Those who perceived a vast body of incipient or covert Loyalists wanted to encourage them, and in general opposed the deliberate use of terrorism. They argued that the great middle ground between active rebellion and active Loyalism should be broadened and strengthened, not cut away, as Lord Carlisle and Major Ferguson would have done. And at the heart of the developing debate over a new British strategy lay the question of the armed Loyalists: What part should they be assigned? Carlisle and Ferguson wanted them unleashed against rebellion; others, who favored a conciliatory approach to Americans in the middle ground, argued for a strictly limited, tightly controlled use of armed Loyalists. The debate never became perfectly straightforward, in part because the proponents of conciliation had to be cautious in speaking of their American allies. But certain groups of armed Loyalists were notorious for engaging in the ugliest kinds of violence, and inevitably that reputation, however justified it may have been, colored the issue. Andrew Elliott, a royal official and later Lieutenant Governor of British-controlled New York, warned that a "destructive war" would be counterproductive, and would simply fill British prisons with victims of what he called "private revenge."[14] Some experienced regular officers, including General Clinton himself, agreed, although they were circumspect in expressing their views.

The war being fought out, day by day and night by night, in dozens of nasty little raids, ambushes, and encounters all over Bergen and Westchester Counties, was complex and confusing; it is almost impossible to state with certainty what actually happened in many controversial episodes—how many atrocities? committed by whom? and why? But it is beyond doubt that the armed Loyalists had a problem, both with their image and with their troops. Again and again, the very orders given by Loyalist officers to their men reveal the seriousness, perhaps the hopelessness, of the problem. "Seize Kill or Apprehend the Rebel Guards," reads one directive for a Tory raid on Closter, New Jersey,

> in that or *any other part of the Country you may March through also every other disaffected person that is known to be aiding or assisting the Rebellion.*

This license to kill every "disaffected person" was tempered by a caveat: "You are not on any Pretence whatever to Hurt or injure any of the well disposed loyal Inhabitants," implying that without explicit orders some of the loyal inhabitants might have been fair game. How seriously the Tory raiders took this warning is suggested by the final sentence of the order, directing that all rebel property seized be divided into equal shares.[15]

Not only did the British Commander-in-Chief and many of his more knowledgeable subordinates know that the nasty little war going on around New York was murderous, they also knew that in other ways it was deeply corrupt. One example can serve. In June 1780 John André, British adjutant general, received a letter from Captain Samuel Hayden of the King's American Rangers, a Loyalist unit. Hayden wrote that his brothers, who had been spying for the King in and around Woodbridge, New Jersey, had been caught by the rebels and were on trial for their lives. On hearing the news, Hayden had led a small detachment of volunteers to Woodbridge and seized the only six men whose testimony could convict his brothers. Now, Hayden wrote, someone was proposing that one of these prisoners and potential witnesses, Thomas Edgar, be exchanged for a Loyalist militia officer in rebel hands. The release of Edgar would endanger his brothers; moreover, Edgar and his fellow prisoners had lost any claim to humane dealing because their Whig friends had executed four of the Tory volunteers captured during the expedition to Wood-bridge.

Without other evidence a historian might well accept Hayden's letter at face value. It conveys a picture of bitter civil war, in which Americans by 1780 had committed themselves to one side or the other, and dealt ruthlessly with their enemies: American brothers spying for the King, caught by a half-dozen Whig neighbors, the neighbors in turn kidnapped by a Tory captain and brother of the spies, Whigs then killing four prisoners in fury at the Tory coup.

But a second letter to André, written a week later by Cortlandt Skinner, chief of the Loyalist New Jersey Volunteers, throws the whole affair into a very different light. Whether the Hayden brothers were employed by the Crown to gather intelligence, Skinner wrote, he had no way of knowing. But he did know, because Captain Hayden had told him, that the brothers were arrested by the rebels for *counterfeiting*. Captain Hayden had been authorized to seize only one man, Barns Burns, also a counterfeiter and the only strong witness against the Hayden brothers. Why Hayden also took six other prisoners, and then let Burns escape, was mysterious,

Cortlandt Skinner, Chief of the Loyalist New Jersey
Volunteers (Courtesy New Jersey Historical Society)

but Skinner thought that Burns' former partnership with the Hayden brothers must somehow be involved, and that the other six men were carried off because the Loyalist soldiers had plundered their property. And the four Tory volunteers captured and hanged by the Whigs, in the first place, were not even authorized to be on the expedition, and, in the second place, had been executed for murder. They had been caught with their pockets full of the money being printed by yet another counterfeiter, whose body had been found by the Whigs. Thomas Edgar, the prisoner whose exchange Captain Hayden opposed, was not a notorious rebel, wrote Skinner, but a man who had accepted royal pardon and signed an oath of allegiance when the British occupied New Jersey in late 1776, and since then had remained quietly at home in Woodbridge, carefully staying out of the war and its politics.

What in one document looks like a clear case of civil war between Whig and Tory, becomes in another a messy affair in which political commitment and revolutionary emotion are less in evidence than personal prudence and blatant criminality. Eventually an inquiry upheld Skinner's version of the affair; but to expect the British actually to punish an enthusiastic American supporter of royal authority like Captain Hayden is to expect too much.[16]

The British debate over the specific role of armed Loyalists in the new strategy of pacification after 1778 was never wholly resolved. It was confused by the fact that both sides of the question sought to exploit the potential of American Loyalism, but each would have exploited a different sector of that potential. The tension and dilemma imbedded in the debate, so visible around New York, remained to plague operations in the Carolinas in 1780 and 1781. Clinton refused to unleash the Tory dogs of war; he sometimes resisted, sometimes evaded pressure to turn the war into one of counterinsurgent terrorism. No doubt his reluctance owed something to a sense of honor, of what a gentleman could—and could not—stoop to in his capacity as a military officer. But certainly his refusal to undertake a full-scale campaign of terrorism stemmed also from a well-documented sense that the chief instrument of terrorism, the armed Loyalists, would poison the American political atmosphere beyond recovery, at best turning the colonies into a larger, more remote, less manageable version of Ireland, where British authority maintained itself by a mixture of corruption, armed force, and a brutal readiness to resort to either on the slightest provocation.

Surely the puzzling question of why the American Revolution never suffered quite the extremes of violence, nor much of its enduring, destructive social effects, finds part of an answer in the way the British chose to wage the war. This choice in turn emerged from the way that British leaders saw at close range Loyalism operating in the lower Hudson Valley.

Guerrilla Activities of
James DeLancey's Cowboys in
Westchester County:
Conventional Warfare or
Self-Interested Freebooting?

Catherine S. Crary

THE DEPREDATIONS and cruelties perpetrated on the inhabitants of Westchester County from 1777 to 1783 are an accepted fact of history[1] kept alive by the inimitable descriptions in James Fenimore Cooper's *The Spy,* Washington Irving's *Wolfert's Roost,* and Timothy Dwight's *Travels.* History can become distorted through these authors' colorful writing. It is easy to remember Irving's vivid sentence: "Neither [Cowboys or Skinners][2] stopped to ask the politics of horse or cow which they drove into captivity; nor, when they wrung the neck of a rooster did they trouble their heads to ascertain whether he were crowing for congress or King George." Thus it is the task of the historian to examine the evidence and to ask who committed the atrocities and whether the guerrilla activities of James DeLancey's Cowboys, as the Westchester Refugees were popularly known, surpassed the bounds of conventional warfare and were simply self-interested freebooting. The experience of Vietnam has shown how hazy are the bounds of conventional warfare and how frequently regular army personnel take advantage of the wartime weakness of civil government to serve their own self-interest.

14

James DeLancey, leader of the Westchester Refugees ("DeLancey's Cowboys"). The artist is unknown. (Courtesy George DeLancey Hanger)

Following the withdrawal of both British and rebel forces after the Battle of White Plains (October 28, 1776), Westchester County became a no-man's land which offered ample opportunity for plunder. Rebel forces drew up a line just above the Croton River, while the British line extended from the Hudson River to the Sound, across the lower part of Yonkers and Eastchester, about two miles above Kings Bridge. Since neither side had the military capability to control the area in between, it was called Neutral Ground, but it was neutral only because the noncombatant farmers wanted to be treated as such and left alone. In this debatable area the Cowboys rustled mainly horses and cattle, while the Skinners, their rebel counterpart, skinned their victims of purses and clothes in addition.

Historians have interpreted in contradictory terms the guerrilla activities of DeLancey's Cowboys, viewing the individuals either as villains or as men of principle. To Otto Hufeland, writing in 1926, both Cowboys and Skinners were "almost without exception . . . the worthless and criminal element of the neighborhood in which they operated . . . governed by neither law or mercy."[3] As for DeLancey's men particularly, he said: "To DeLancey and his native partisan corps, more than to any other enemy organization, was·due the terrible devastation and suffering which nearly destroyed and depopulated the 'Neutral Ground.'"[4]

On the other hand, more recently, historian James Pickering considered the Cowboys as "dedicated Loyalists forced by their militant Whig neighbors to flee their homes and seek refuge with the British. Many of the Cowboys were principled men fighting to regain their homes and their rights."[5] For Pickering, it was the Skinners who were "outright freebooters, . . . small independent gangs of militiamen or whaleboatmen who were not above spending their leisure hours in pursuit of ill-gotten plunder."[6] He suggests that the Cowboys were dubbed outlaws and villains because of the prejudice of early American historians.

With guerrilla warfare and terrorism against civilians the subject of frequent headlines in the last decade and the use of guerrillas or partisans an accepted tactic of warfare throughout the nineteenth and twentieth centuries, it may be appropriate to revisit the Neutral Ground and review the activities of DeLancey's Cowboys more objectively than did early historians or Hufeland. Were they the principal perpetrators of the criminal acts against noncombatant farmers and their families in the county? Were they acting under military authority in accord with conventional warfare under the laws of war? Do they deserve the stamp of inhuman buccaneers or were they less villainous, wanton, and self-interested than they have been painted in the past?

Six other groups besides the Cowboys operated in the Neutral Ground—British, American, and French armies, privateers, common thieves and criminals, and the Skinners —yet, as DeLancey wrote to Sir Guy Carleton, every irregularity committed in the County was indiscriminately charged to the Cowboys.[7] Many witnesses have told about the ravages of other bands. Washington wrote Governor William Livingston of New Jersey, November 7, 1776, of the ravages of the British army as it moved through Westchester, saying: "They have treated all here without discrimination. The distinction of Whig and Tory has been lost here in one general scene of ravage and desolation." To General Nathanael Greene he added: "Many helpless women had even the shifts taken from their backs by the soldiers' wives after the great plunderers had done."[8] Again, Samuel Lyon told how Fred Donaldson, an American cruising as a privateer under a commission from Governor Clinton, often exceeded his powers and landed and ravaged on Long Island and Westchester.[9] As to common thieves and criminals, Lyon said that two brothers named Quail, as well as many others who deserted or were discharged from Stephen Moylan's Company, turned robbers and plundered the farmers who had entertained them.[10] Depositions of Westchester inhabitants testified that officers of the American army robbed them of furniture, household items, and clothes, as well as horses and cattle, for their own private use.[11] Again a French officer, identified as Baron Cromot du Bourg, an aide to Rochambeau, wrote in his diary, July 23, 1781: "At my great surprise many depredations were committed by the French. The hussars pillaged many houses and even the grenadiers and chasseurs had a hand in it. This conduct was severely censured and they were punished by several hundred blows of the stick."[12] Joseph Odell of Greenburgh also told how a detachment of Lauzun's cavalry called at the smithy of Elijah Vincent's brother in Eastchester and asked him to shoe their horses. He refused as it was Sunday. A fight ensued and the smithy was killed. Elijah Vincent vowed revenge and later killed a French captain in retaliation and took his watch.[13] The Skinners likewise robbed and murdered.[14]

More important than the ravages which can be attributed to others is the evidence that the Cowboys were acting under British military authority and were assigned essential military tasks. The record of their enlistment in regular army units, as well as their military service in the war, may be found in the Loyalist Transcripts, in the thirty or forty memorials to the Crown claiming compensation for their losses. Of the thirty examined, twenty-nine men said they were born in Westchester or Dutchess Counties and almost all had served in a regular army unit, such as the New York Volunteers, the Queen's Rangers, the King's American Regiment, or the Engineer or Quartermaster Departments, before volunteering to join DeLancey's troops. Invariably they wrote: "Joined the British Army" and the officers added "commissioned by Governor Tryon," who was Commander-in-Chief of the Provincial Forces. Not only were DeLancey's men properly enrolled, but they were also under military control and discipline under the chain of command. They were duly authorized to conduct guerrilla activities which would serve the interest of British military strategy. Their tasks were proper and essential in organized warfare, that is, to obtain forage and provisions, to keep communications open, to protect the vital post at Kings Bridge, and to take prisoners for exchange. They were drilled with care by British officers from New York and carried arms openly.[15] DeLancey's horsemen were generally in uniform with military hats, although footsoldiers, like the rebel militia, were not as a rule properly outfitted.[16] Thus they were lawful combatants and entitled to be treated as prisoners of war if captured.[17]

The memorial of Captain Samuel Kipp of Northcastle (Chappaqua), for example, illustrates the Cowboys' view of their role. He said he joined the Queen's Rangers soon after the Battle of Long Island and served during the fall campaign of 1776 in Westchester. In November 1779 he was duly commissioned by Governor Tryon as a lieutenant in Captain Knapp's Troop of Light Horse, part of DeLancey's corps. Not only did Kipp consider he was as much a commissioned officer in the King's army as any other officer in the Loyalist brigades, but also he considered his assignment a proper task of the army and not pillaging for personal gain. He wrote of DeLancey's corps:

They occupied the Post in the Front of the Lines of the British Army during the whole war, without Pay or any other Reward than a consciousness of doing their Duty as faithful subjects. That by means of their exertions in that Situation the important Post of Kings Bridge was kept free from the Insults of the Enemy and the Communication with the Country [kept] so perfectly open as to enable the Inhabitants to supply the Magazines with a great proportion of Provision and Forage; that they made frequent and successful exertions into the Enemy's Lines; that in the course of the war they captured so many prisoners as enabled them not only to exchange their own Men but to furnish upwards of 500 for the release of the Royal Army and at the close of the war they had the Paroles of above 200 Prisoners more. . . .[18]

DeLancey's own memorial, April 3, 1783, directed to Sir Guy Carleton, detailed the services of his five hundred men, who served without either pay or clothing, and claimed that the discipline of his men surpassed that of other military bodies. It read:

That by Means of their Service the Enemy has been constantly kept at such a Distance from King's Bridge as to render that Post perfectly secure & to keep up a Communication with the Country People for the Supply of the Magazines & Markets at New York. That the Enemy have been repelled in every Attempt to destroy the People under your Memorialist's Command; & that in the many Engagements which he has had with them your Memorialist has been so fortunate as to capture a Number of Prisoners sufficient not only for the Exchange of his own Men, but also for the Release of about five hundred British Prisoners.

That your Memorialist has in the Course of his Services repeatedly received the Thanks of the Commander in Chief & of those General Officers under whom he has had the Honor to serve.

That he has always endeavoured to maintain the strictest & most exemplary Discipline in his Corps & has gone in that respect much beyond what has ever been practised in other Bodies constituted in a similar Manner.

That your memorialist has at all Times exerted the most anxious & unwearied Attention to preserve the Property of the Inhabitants in the Country & afford them every Protection, by which Means he is well convinced that he has acquired & maintained the firm & general Attachment at least of such of them as were loyally disposed. But that he now finds to his great Mortification, that there is a Number of People, irritated at his Zeal & Services in the Cause of Government, who secretly endeavour to prejudice him in your Excellency's Opinion by collecting in an underhand Manner, Depositions respecting every Irregularity committed in the County of Westchester & its Vicinity; which are indiscriminately charged against the Refugees under his Command tho' most of them have originated from People who have no Connection with that Corps. [19]

DeLancey felt that his reputation had hitherto been unimpeached. The rest of his corps, as Bolton comments, "considered the rapine by which they subsisted . . . lawful and honorable."[20] Governor Tryon said they came from the colony's elite.[21] McDonald too, referring to both Cowboys and Skinners, wrote: "Ordinarily they piqued themselves upon the point of honor and were generous to captives. Every steed . . . was considered a lawful prize; . . . the urgent wants of the King or the necessities of the States gave a sanction to such captures. With this exception, the hands of many, perhaps most of them, were unstained by plunder."[22]

One further important question is whether they observed the laws of war as recognized in the late eighteenth century, and codified by Emerich de Vattel, the writer on international law closest in time to the Revolution. In *The Law of Nations*, which appeared in 1758, he stressed the principle that natural law was superior to man-made law and endeavoured to reconcile the laws of war to man's natural rights. However, almost every law discussed is accompanied by a qualification. For example, he writes: "Women, children, the sick and aged . . . are enemies who make no resistance and consequently give us no right to treat their persons ill or use any violence against them much less to take away their lives. This is so plain a maxim of justice and humanity that at present every nation in the least civilized acquiesces in it." Vattel then adds "unless they have committed acts of hostility."[23] Again he writes: "On an enemy's submitting and delivering up his arms, we cannot with justice take away his life. . . . [However,] there is one case where life may be denied an enemy who surrenders. This is when the enemy has been guilty of . . . a violation of the laws of war. Denial of quarter is . . . punishment which the injured party has a right to inflict."[24] He then asks whether prisoners who cannot be kept or fed may be put to death or should they be sent back. His answer is: "When our safety is incompatible with that of our enemy, . . . it is out of all question but that in cool blood a great number of prisoners should be put to death."[25]

As to plunder, Vattel states: "A nation has a right to deprive the enemy of his possessions and goods, of everything which may augment his forces and enable him to make war." These are broad rights and significant exceptions to humanitarian laws of war, especially when noncombatant readily acted as informants and guides. The extenuating circumstances in incidents which seemed a violation of the laws of war may never be known, for many of the men could not answer the charges, banished and discredited, as they were, by the victors before all the circumstances could be weighed.

The interviews of John McDonald with elderly residents of Westchester from 1844–1851 furnish some eyewitness material concerning the Cowboys' treatment of noncombatants and their methods of warfare. Although some persons interviewed tell of unnecessary cruelty and blame individual members of DeLancey's corps, the interviews reveal a surprising lack of condemnation of the Cowboys and of vindictiveness against them for ruthless acts perpetrated on their families. In fact, Andrew Corsa, one of the Westchester Guides for the rebels, who accompanied McDonald on his interviews, described Nehemiah Brown, an officer in DeLancey's troop, as "a humane man," who "treated his prisoners well."[26] Captain Samuel Kipp and Lieutenant James Kipp of Chappaqua were also described as humane and gentlemenly and as leaders under whom the men loved to serve. Samuel Chadeayne of Yorktown considered Captain Gilbert Totten as a "remarkably well-built and soldierly-looking man, honorable and high-principled."[27] Mrs. Daniel Edwards characterized Major Thomas Huggeford as a "large, fleshy, middle-aged man, active and humane."[28]

Chadeayne told of an incident in 1781 when discipline broke down and DeLancey responded by expelling a private, James Totten, for robbing and killing an innocent French officer. DeLancey said he was a disgrace to the corps. Chadeayne wrote: "Totten had come up to Colonel [Christopher] Greene's with a flag when for some reason he was coolly and slightingly received . . . and felt so much neglected and insulted that at parting he let fall this threat: 'Colonel Greene shall before long repent the treatment I have this day received.'" When the

French left White Plains in 1781 some sick soldiers were left at North Castle and a French surgeon went down daily from Yorktown to see them. He was waylaid by James Totten, James Tillott, and two others about a mile from Pine's Bridge and robbed of his clothes, money, and watch. The robbers then played a game of "all fours" to decide who should kill him and it was done. When Totten appeared at Morrisania in the victim's clothes and boasted of the deed he received a sharp reproof from DeLancey: "Totten, you think you have accomplished an honorable and brave exploit in taking the life of a poor French doctor who made no resistance. You are a disgrace to the Refugees and I want to see you no more. Take my advice and withdraw from this place for rely upon it if you don't the rebels will spare no effort or expense to hang you. . . ."[29]

Another incident was told by Benjamin Brush concerning a DeLancey trooper named Josiah Gaines. He was wounded near Round Hill and Dr. Belcher cured him, only to have the convalescent steal his horse. When DeLancey heard about the ingratitude he made Gaines pay his benefactor the full value of the horse.[30] There were other instances when DeLancey gave protection to local farmers. When horses, oxen, and cattle were taken from the people at Horseneck for the use of the British army, DeLancey ordered that each family should keep one cow for their own use.

The most surprising testimony came from Lydia Vail of Somers, the granddaughter of Richard Davenport whose house near Pines Bridge was used as Colonel Greene's head-quarters. Greene and about twenty other rebel soldiers were killed in a surprise attack by some two hundred Cowboys at the Davenport house, May 14, 1781. The latter were accused of massacre and barbarity. Greene's men had agreed to surrender in return for quarter, but someone fired from the Davenport house provoking the Cowboys to attack and give no quarter. At the Griffen house two miles away, Captain Samuel Knapp and Lieutenant Gilbert Totten also promised quarter and good treatment in return for surrender. The conditions were ac-cepted when two blacks in the rebel regiment fired, provoking further slaughter. Lydia Vail exonerated these men, saying: "After all the circumstances and the surprise at Davenport's house came to be known Colonel DeLancey and the Refugees were not blamed. The impetuosity and indiscretion of a single individual, caused probably all the bloodshed at my grand-father's. . . ."[31]

In summary, the guerrilla activities of DeLancey's Cowboys were a type of military action, carried on by a band of irregular soldiers, similar to the actions of Ethan Allen's Green Moun-tain Boys, or of Francis Marion's and Andrew Pickens' bands in the South in 1780–1781. In fact, Pickens' regiment was to be paid by plundering Loyalists. Marion's most recent biog-rapher, Robert D. Bass, wrote of his methods: "He shot pickets, retaliated from ambush, failed to honor flags of truce, and knowingly violated international law."[32] DeLancey, how-ever, tried to operate within the laws of war and maintain discipline over his subordinates to observe the same. When one of his men was guilty of murder or other crimes he was punished. The Cowboys' reputation for brutality derived partly from the cavalry's use of the saber as a more effective weapon for mounted men than a gun and partly from the fact that hit-run tactics often precluded the taking of prisoners and extending to them the humane treatment prescribed by the laws of war.

This examination of the objectives and conduct of DeLan-cey's Cowboys does not justify a whitewash of their reputation or praise for their methods of warfare. It does suggest, how-ever, that the opprobrium heaped upon them at the close of the war went to extremes and was not justified on the basis of the evidence in their memorials and in the McDonald Interviews. Yet it is not surprising that the fugitive losers, who could not answer the charges of wanton cruelty made against them, were denounced and blamed for the suffering and devastation in Westchester County.

Frederick Philipse III of Westchester County: A Reluctant Loyalist

Jacob Judd

IN RECENT WRITINGS concerned with those colonials who chose to remain loyal to the Crown during the American revolutionary struggle, historians have emphasized political ideology, party factionalism, and church affiliation as some of the outstanding factors which helped determine their choice of loyalty. Others stressed that allegiances related to social and political position helped formulate the ultimate decision as to whether one supported the rebellious colonists or not. A predetermined set of characteristics, it has been argued, could establish a predictable pattern of behavior in the Revolutionary Era.

If, as in the case of New York province, an individual happened to be a member of the Anglican church, was a follower of the so-called DeLancey Faction in politics, and held some governmental post, then he eventually would, most likely, come to be counted in the ranks of the Loyalists. And, if such a person happened to own extensive property, he most assuredly would have become a partisan of the Crown. Furthermore, it is contended, sentiment concerning such a political stance would have coalesced shortly after the close of the Seven Years' War when Great Britain severely modified her imperialistic controls over the American colonies.[1]

As is so often the case when a wide brush is swashed across a canvas a number of blemishes can be hidden from view but the underlying imperfections remain. The imperfections in the behavioral theory of patterned Loyalist adherence need to be revealed and examined in full view.

In every characteristic New Yorkers were unique and cannot readily be placed into predetermined categories. There is ample evidence that in New York the post-1763 difficulties did not create an overt separation into distinct political groups which either supported or denied Crown authority. New York Provincial leaders were united behind the concept that the Crown had erred in its attempt to compel colonial tax support with the Revenue Acts of 1764 and 1765; but, at the same time, they adhered to the view that the Crown's authority must be recognized. An effort to predict on the basis of their political stance as of 1765 who would become a patriot in the later struggle would have been well nigh a hopeless task. As late as January 1776 a substantial number of the political elite were still wavering in their allegiance. It was events outside the Province which finally compelled them to reach fateful decisions. The creation of the two Congresses, Lexington and Concord, Bunker and Breed's Hill, and the publication of *Common Sense* brought some urgency to their decision-making. Most New Yorkers did not appear to know where they actually stood in regard to Crown control until the writing of the Declaration of Independence. In fact, New York did not ratify the Declaration until July 9, at a point when it realized that it had to join her sister states in the ensuing struggle or stand against them alone.[2]

To speak of a Tory or Court party as existing in New York in the 1760s is an exercise in futility. It is not until after Great Britain's violent reaction to the Boston Tea Party that some New Yorkers began to act, apparently in concert, in seeking to subvert the activities of extralegal bodies in the province and on the continent. Attempting to punish Boston for its willful destruction of property, Great Britain enacted the Grievance Acts. In answer to that move, a call came forth for the colonies to send representatives to an assembly wherein all the colonies would be represented and where they could discuss what countermeasures might be instituted as their concerted answer to the Grievance Acts. It was at that point, beginning in

John Wollaston the Younger, an English artist, painted this portrait, which is probably of Frederick Philipse III. (Courtesy New-York Historical Society)

1774, that a group of New York legislators consistently voted
during the next few years to thwart the establishment of the
Continental Congresses and New York's participation in those
bodies. We are aware of the "conservative" attitude assumed
by the New York representatives in those bodies and how
reluctantly the province itself moved in the direction of rebellion. New York cannot be classified as being in the vanguard of
the revolutionary spirit.[3]

Perhaps, by focusing on one individual it may be possible to
analyze some forces which operated in determining the political fate of an influential person in that very confused era.

Frederick Philipse III, possessor of a great name and vast
lands in New York, had been an esteemed member of the New
York Assembly since 1750. The family, of which he was the
head, exemplified what ambition could accomplish in this land
of opportunity. The founder of the New York branch was a
Dutchman, Vrydrich Flypsen, who arrived in New Amster-
dam in the 1640s. Employed as a carpenter by the Dutch West
India Company, Flypsen seized every opportunity opened to
him under the Charter of Freedoms and Exemptions of the
Company. He had already set himself on the path of commerce, when the Dutch province fell to the English.

Flypsen was one of the first to take the Oath of Allegiance to
King Charles II and soon anglicized his name to Frederick
Philipse, but continued to use VF as his business monogram.
His ascendancy to financial power was rapid. Within a short
time his ships were traversing the known commercial routes of
the world, he had become a councillor to the governor, and he
had risen to social prominence. His acquisitiveness then
turned to land. After all, in a developing country there is
nothing more valuable than land which can be turned to productive use.

Between the early 1670s and 1693, Philipse pieced together an estate extending from the northern reaches of Manhattan Island to the Croton River on the north, and extending
inland to the Bronx River as its eastern boundary. This vast
estate of over 90,000 acres was officially recognized as the

Manor of Philipsburg in 1693 and Frederick received the designation of Lord of the Manor.

The trade and land empire created by Frederick was expanded by his son, Adolph. The landed properties were enlarged by Adolph's acquisition of lands further north of Philipsburg Manor, in the area now known as Putnam County. In addition, the Philipse-controlled vessels carried on a trade more lucrative than ever before. It was this family wealth and position which was passed on to Adolph's nephew, Frederick II, the father of our subject.

Frederick III, who inherited the property in 1751, apparently did not devote himself to the mercantile trade as had his ancestors, but concentrated on private banking activities and land ownership. Whereas the earlier Philipses had not been too concerned with intensive development of their landholdings, Frederick III had become aware of its agricultural potential since the market for food products had expanded commensurately with the growth of the City of New York. Westchester lands had significantly increased in value from the earlier decades of the eighteenth century because of their proximity to the city. Whereas large landholdings had primarily represented social status for the possessor in an earlier day, such tracts soon became the basis for wealth in their own right.

The earlier Philipses concentrated on the development of overseas commercial activities and secondarily amassed land for prestige as well as for long-term investment capabilities. Frederick III dropped the commercial aspects of the family business and relied instead on the income his lands could produce. He was not a plantation owner in the Southern sense of operating a vast self-contained economic unit. Rather, he relied on tenant farmers, who would pay a royalty for the use of his land, to develop it. Unique in the relationship between Philipse and his tenants was the absence of written contracts which delineated the rents they were to pay. Apparently, an unwritten arrangement was understood by both parties wherein the rent would not be changed on a given property as long as the agreeing parties were alive. Thus Philipse could

modify a rental if the tenant farmer died and a son subsequently occupied the same land or house; or if a Philipse
died, then the heir could alter everyone's rent. The records
demonstrate that Frederick III had not sought to change the
rents since he inherited the lands in the early 1750s. Furthermore, the relationship between Philipse and his tenants
seemed to be extremely amicable.

While the Livingston and Van Cortlandt estates were strife-
torn by tenant complaints and uprisings in the 1750s and 1760s,
Philipsburg Manor continued in a placid manner. Strangely
enough, this pleasant relationship between tenants and landlord might have helped create the aura of suspicion surround-
ing Philipse's motivations, which led to his difficulties with the
revolutionary government. The New York Committee of
Safety leveled the charge against Philipse that they "verily
believe that the shameful defection of the inhabitants of that
County is in great measure owing to his influence."[4] Numbers
of Westchester inhabitants had opted to remain loyal subjects
of the Crown and a reason had to be found. Some thought
the obvious cause must have been Philipse's control over his
tenants.

Philipse lived a relatively calm and retiring life up to the
years of turmoil. Characterized by the Rev. Timothy Dwight as
a "worthy and respectable man, not often excelled in personal
and domestic amiableness. . . . This gentleman was proprietor
of the neighboring country to a great extent, and one of the
wealthiest inhabitants of the province of New York."[5] He
resided in a mansion in the Yonkers section of the Manor of
Philipsburg surrounded by orchards, gardens, and a host of
servants and slaves. This "well tempered, amiable man" had a
penchant for "gardening, planting, etc., and employed much
time and money in that way," so said his erstwhile revolutionary adversary, John Jay.[6]

A colonel in the Provincial Militia, he routinely attended
sessions of the New York Assembly where he rarely spoke but
was regarded as a solid member. Then his world suddenly took
a dramatic turn with events occurring outside the province. He

was appointed to the New York Committee of Correspondence in January 1774, and voted with the majority in adopting a Declaration of Grievances on March 13, 1775. In that vote he joined such later revolutionary stalwarts as George Clinton, Philip Schuyler, and Philip Livingston in stating that England's Declaratory Act was a "Grievance," and that the Tea Act was a grievance for it revoked "that system of Rights and Privileges on which the Government of the colonies hath been established; as it deprives the Legislatures of the colonies, of the Rights and Privileges which they always, before the passing that Act, have been esteemed intitled to, and, of Right, enjoy equal with the people of Great Britain."[7] He balked, however, at the need of appointing delegates to the Second Continental Congress.[8]

In May 1775 a number of the Assembly members sent an Address to General Thomas Gage in which they declared their ardent wish "for a cordial Reconciliation" but warned that they had become increasingly alarmed at the actions of the British forces in Massachusetts. "Alarmed as we are by the ruinous Consequences which must inevitably follow the prosecution of hostile Measures, and anxiously affected with the Calamities of an Unnatural Civil War, we are induced most earnestly to entreat your Excellency in behalf of Colonies (which however tenacious of their Rights and Liberties, and Jealous of every Infringement of them, can be exceeded in Loyalty and Affection for our most gracious Sovereign by None of his Subjects) that your Excellency will as far as may be consistant with your Duty, immediately Order a Cessation of further Hostilities. . . ."[9] Among the signatories were Pierre Van Cortlandt, soon to become the State's first Lieutenant Governor, and Frederick Philipse.

At what point in the ensuing rapid events did Philipse cry, "Hold, enough?" The final moment of truth came to Frederick in 1776 when the inhabitants of New York were urged to take an oath of allegiance to the revolutionary cause. He at first hesitated and then rallied other Westchesterites in support of the Crown. "Actuated by the firmest principles of loyalty in

attachment to the British Government," said Frederick
Philipse, "he exerted his influence to prevent it, and particularly in the Spring of 1776, he convened a large number of the
Freeholders and inhabitants of the Town of West Chester and
prevailed on them to enter into an association to preserve the
peace and to support the local government. . . ."[10]

This action brought down the wrath of the Committee of
Safety who, on June 27, 1776, resolved to question his loyalty.
Following this, Philipse apparently was placed under some
form of house arrest until August 9 when he was seized and
taken by military escort to New Rochelle in Westchester
County. This area was further removed from possible military
activity than was Yonkers, Philipse's main place of residence.
Frederick Philipse did not view his effort at rallying support for
the Crown from among Westchester residents as being inimical to the American cause. His appeal to the New York Committee of Safety left it clear that he felt he had been falsely
accused.

To the Honourable the Congress
or Committee of Safety
of the State of New York
The Memorial of Federick Phillips

Humbly Sheweth

That on the 9th Day of August Last your Memorialist was, by
order of his Excellency General Washington taken into Custody at his own house, and immediately sent Prisoner from
thence to New Rochelle, where he was closely confined
under Guard—That soon after, being removed to Connecticut, a Parole, (a copy whereof is herunto Annexed) was
presented to him which he signed, and agreeable thereto,
has ever since been confin'd to this Town, and a small district
round it,—That your Memorialist has thus been deprived of
his liberty without any particular matter being alledged
against him, or ever having an opportunity of offering anything in his own defence—That conscious of his having
committed no offence against the Community of which he is

a Member, nor taken any part in the present unhappy Contest, which could in anyways be construed unfriendly to the General interest of America, he cannot help thinking that General Washington must have been induced to take this step in consequence of some Misrepresentations—That he has already suffered great hardships and inconveniences and if not permitted to return to his own house before the severety of the winter sets in must still suffer many more, which, in his advanced stage of life and infirm state of Health he is ill calculated to undergo—But that even all the personal inconveniences he has felt and is likely farther to feel, if not soon relieved, are far from making so deep an impression on his mind as the Circumstance of being seperated from his wife and Numerous family, and thereby prevented from Superintending his own affairs, particularly the Education of his Children whose tender years require the most watchfull attention of a Parents Care—Your Memorialist therefore Prays, that your Honours will be pleased to take his case under Consideration and afford him relief by restoring him again to his liberty or if that cannot be granted at present, that he may be indulged with Leave to reside at his own house (with such limits thereto as you may think fit to prescribe) under a parole similar to that which he has already given

All which is humbly Submitted[11]

During the next few weeks, Philipse wrote a series of letters of which five are still extant, to his wife, Elizabeth Williams Philipse, in which he depicted the difficulties and trauma of his situation (following this chapter).[12]

In the letter dated 22 August, Frederick made the interesting statement that "I am concious that I have done nothing (upon the Strictest Examination) Inimical to the Liberty's of My Country. . . . " This is a plaint which he repeated in his Memorial to the Committee of Safety in December, and which demonstrates that he regarded his actions as being in keeping with the preservation of colonial liberties.

While absent from his home, Elizabeth Philipse was having difficulty with the American forces who were sequestering horses and cattle. George Washington wrote to her in October that, "The Misfortunes of War, and the unhappy circumstances frequently attendant thereon to Individuals, are more to be lamented than avoided; but it is the duty of every one, to alleviate these as much as possible. Far be it from me then, to add to the distresses of a Lady, who, I am but too sensible, must already have suffered much uneasiness, if not inconvenience, on account of Colonel Philips's absence."[13]

General Charles Lee was not as cordial to her when he answered her request that Philipse-owned cattle not be moved to Peekskill in late November 1776. Lee declared that the "Hessian Marauders" will seize all her cattle and that he had to prevent her possessions from falling into the "Hands of those Ruffian Hirelings." Still having trouble maintaining her stock, she again exchanged letters with him and this time he warned, "Neutrals in civil Country can by no means be suffered—those that do not take a positive active part with their Country [shall be treated] as enemies—their whole stock shall be siezed & their houses burnt." He added that he hoped that he could count "Mrs. Philips amongst the friends of her Country—and not amongst its Enemies. . . ."[14]

Frederick Philipse was eventually escorted to Governor Jonathan Trumbull's home in Lebanon, Connecticut, where he remained until granted a parole by that State's Council of Safety on December 20. Under its terms he could return home but he was not to give any intelligence to the enemy, take up arms against the United States, or to say or do anything inimical to the American cause.[15] His own state's Committee of Safety was not as lenient for they asserted that his returning home, "would put it in the power of a professed enemy of the American cause not only further to disaffect the inhabitants of West-Chester County, but to put many of them in arms against the United States of America."[16]

Shortly afterwards, Frederick Philipse along with his wife and children sought refuge behind the British lines in New

York City. By violating his parole he became a marked man as far as the rebellious Americans were concerned. Suspicions against him were further increased when he soon became counted as a member of Governor William Tryon's inner circle. General William Howe's secretary reported: "Governor Tryon, Col. [Frederick] Philipse, Mr. [Henry] White, etc., dined with us today. Philipse had long been confined by the Rebels in Connecticut, but was lately released."[17]

Despite or contrary to Philipse's supposed influence over his manor tenants, there were many outstanding rebels among his tenants. The two Van Tassels, Peter and Cornelius, were seized by a British raiding party in November 1777 and their house put to the torch. The American commander, Samuel H. Parsons, complained to General Tryon over the misbehavior of the British forces during that raid and warned that, "'Tis not my Inclination, Sir, to war in this manner against the Inhabitants within your Lines who suppose themselves within the Protection of the King. But Necessity will oblige me to retaliate in Kind, upon your Friends, to compel the Exercise of that Justice which Humanity Used to dictate." And, as for Frederick Philipse, the General added, "You cannot be insensible tis every Day in my Power to destroy the Buildings belonging to Col. Philips & Mr. Delancey."[18] Even though Philipsburg Manor was the site of much activity by both armies during the entire war, the remaining buildings seem to have been spared, possibly because of their utility to both opposing forces.

While Frederick was living rather comfortably in New York City, the revolutionary government of the State of New York decreed in November 1779 that, "divers persons holding or claiming property within this State, have voluntarily been adherent to the said King, his fleets and armies, enemies to this State, . . . by reason whereof, the said persons have severally justly forfeited all right to the protection of this State, and to the benefit of the laws under which such property is held or claimed; and whereas the public justice and safety of this State absolutely require, that the most notorious offenders should be immediately hereby convicted and attainted of the offence aforesaid, in order to work a forfeiture of their respective estates, and vest the same in the people of this State. . . ." Among a distinguished group of prominent citizens so attainted was Frederick Philipse, Esquire, "now or late of the county of Westchester."[19] Until that time, Philipse had been receiving the rents on several of his properties while he and his family remained in the city. The Act of Forfeiture prevented him from further rent collections, at least those that the State government could stop. His major source of income had ceased. As a result, he applied to the British Commander-in-Chief, Guy Carleton, for an allowance. A sum of £200 per annum was subsequently awarded to him in December 1782 because of his "having been obliged to leave his estate and property on account of his attachment to his Majesty's Government."[20]

Philipse remained in the city until the conclusion of hostilities at which time he debarked for London. While in London he was visited by a New Yorker, John Watts, who reported, "I saw Col. & Mrs. Philips yesterday, bravely. . . ."[21] Frederick had no choice but to be brave over his plight. Failing in health, his claims for recompense from the Loyalist Commissioners were then slowly working their way through the maze of necessary hearings, witnesses and filing of financial statements. He sought a total of £40,216.18. sterling as compensation for the loss of his manorial holdings, city property and outstanding bonds. While this claim was being processed, Frederick Philipse III died on April 30, 1785, in Chester, England. The Commissioners subsequently awarded his heirs some £53,000 sterling and the widow an annual allowance of £200 sterling. The claims were seemingly not too inflated because the New York Commissioners of Forfeiture received £107,532 in New York currency as settlement of the estate. Even at a post-war rate of inflation, the Philipse holdings were well worth a minimum of £53,766 sterling.

A comprehensive collection of the original documents relating to the claims of the Philipse family appears in the Appendix (pages 95–151).

Why did Frederick Philipse choose loyalism? Some contemporaries averred that his wife was the persuasive force, others that he might have passed military secrets to the British and therefore was afraid to remain in Westchester, and still others have declared that it was inevitable that he remain loyal to Crown authority. With the war rapidly engulfing his property he had to make a choice: either move further upcountry in New York into the area controlled by the rebels, or seek refuge in the strongest British occupied region—New York City. Understanding his political proclivities as of that time, it is no surprise then that he chose New York City. Whether this was a correct move can still be a subject of debate. Even the Claims Commissioners declared that, "There is only one thing for which we cannot commend him. He broke his parole which was the occasion (& perhaps the just occasion) of his being proscribed, but when we consider that he did all that to serve this country, and perhaps it is an additional reason to give him a comfortable support." Whatever the ultimate reason, he lost a great deal as a result. Two sons were killed in the war, his estates were gone, all that his family had stood for in New York was at an end, and most likely his own demise was hastened.

A source of controversy among historians up to the present day concerns the motivation of the New York revolutionary government in confiscating the Philipse estate, dividing it into farm lots, and then selling it to former tenants who could demonstrate their allegiance to the revolutionary cause as well as to land speculators. Why should this estate have been singled out for such treatment? After all, Philipse could not be compared to members of the DeLancey family who organized and led Loyalist military units throughout the conflict, or to Samuel Seabury, a Loyalist propagandist active in New York. Was it a reaction to the large number of Loyalists who came from Westchester County? Was Frederick Philipse being punished for the sentiments of his tenants? The discussions on the subject will continue, and unless more direct documentary material is uncovered, we most likely will never really know what factors led to this action.

Another line of thought, originating with John Franklin
Jameson, dealt with New York's effort to democratize its landholding system as an aftermath of the Revolution. It has been
pointed out by many historians that the replacement of one
landowner by 287 independent farmowners was rather distinct
in its democratic characteristics. Most recently, a student of
New York history has declared that petitions sent by former
Philipse tenants to the State legislature in 1779 and in 1782
urged a distribution of former Loyalist lands. "Whether or not
the state based its actions upon these and other similar petitions is difficult to estimate."[22] The same author concludes,
however, that "the tenants did benefit for many leaseholders or
those related to them participated in the sales." For the
Philipses, this was a moot point.

The crushing blow which had been rendered this family was
recognized by a Polish writer who visited New York in 1798.
Commenting on the scenery along the Hudson River, Julian
Niemcewicz stated: "I saw amongst others a pretty house with
a large and beautiful garden. It belonged once to the Filips
[sic] family, which at the time of the Revolution naturally took
the side of the English and had its estate completely confiscated. Examples of this severity, this confiscation, are rare
in America. . . ."[23]

LETTERS FROM FREDERICK PHILIPSE III

TO HIS WIFE, ELIZABETH WILLIAMS PHILIPSE

1

[August 11, 1776]

My Dearest Life

Tomorrow we are to leave this place but am Afraid we shall not be able for want of waggons to take most of our baggage there are none to be found in this part of the Country and am heartily sick of this vile place I should therefore be greatly Obliged to you If your could get Abram Odell to hire Jacob Post waggon with his own horses to Carry up my baggage as far as New haven where I can procure another and send this back Abram must set of by day break as we promised to meet the Officer who is to Conduct us to Governor Trumbull and one Cap^{tn} Prentice who is known to Mr Babcock he is of New haven and behaves with remarkable politeness and civility he shewed us his orders from Gen Washington which are remarkable kind and favourable to us we are to travel at our Leasure and not to hurry us in the least and to provide for us the best Accommodations on the road & to keep an Acc^t of all the Expence on the road in short I could not have wished for better orders and am verry positive the Capt will keep up to them but loose no time in sending Abram up by Day break to morrow I have ordered the Express to Call on Abram and bring him to you

I have nothing more to write but to beg you to keep by all means and dont Doubt all will end well yet the General has given us the Strongest Assurance that asoon as the Battle is over let who will get the Victory we shall be Imediately released — God of his Infinite goodness take you and our Children Into his protection and am my Dearest Love

Your Affection^t hus^d
FP

Sunday afternoon
My love to all my friends.

2

My Dearest Life

I return you many thanks for your kind favour and have wrote you so late that nothing worthy notice has hapened. Since I hope you have procured me Posts waggon and sent it of before this reaches you for I am really tired & sick of this Filthy place the house is Crowded from morning to night with four Company's of Militia that are parading here for what purpose I cannot learn but are verry Noisey Companions If the waggon was Arrived I would set of Immediately rain or shine I am thank verry well and in tolerable Spirits and should be more so If I Could once get rid of this vile place. M^r· Pintard has been remarkable Civil & kind to me gave a General Invitation to his house both to lodge & Dine M^r· Abramse and M^r· John Myers have Likewise been remarkably Civil and generous In their Invitations but for some reasons would not go abroad. I shall upon all future occasions Inclose my Letters to you to the Care of M^r· Isaac Williams at West Chester who has promised to take Care of them and all your Letters to Me direct Inclosed to M^r· John Porit merchant at Norwich the Gentleman than M^r· Babcock recommended me to — and get M^r· Babcock to Direct them. I[f] any news should come to your knowledge write it on the Inside of the Cover of your Letters not with Ink but the Juice of a Lemon and I shall do the same, My best regards to good M^r· Babcock and my verry friend M^r· Shaw and M^rs· Shaw and M^rs· Morris M^rs· Ludlow &c My love to polly & Fred: thank them for their Letter Shall answer them asoon as I arrive at the place of Exile. My Love to the Children and Charge them from me to be Dutyfull to you and mind their Study's and be verry Obedient And pay the greatest attention to M^r· Babcock and not open their lipps about the times. God bless you My Dearest and may he strengthen and support us with Grace to bear his Dispensations with resignation to his Divine will is the sincere prayer of —

Your affectionate husband
FP

N: Rochelle
14th Augs^t 1776

I shall write to M^r· Williams the overseer as soon as I am settled Excuse this Incoherent Letter as there is such a noise I cannot write with attention.

3

[August, 1776]

Words Cannot Express the Anxciety I was under Last night when I heard—fireing and Saw the lights of the fireships one of our Company hear'd a Cannon we all Imediately got out of bed and sat at the door for two hours untill the firing and lights Ceased and disappeared but words Cannot Express my uneasyness I never Closed my Eyes but remained in that State untill Diamond came with your kind Letter which was a reviving Cordial and made me very easy — the Almighty will I trust take us into his holy protection that we may meet once more in peace & Security.

our Departure is now determined we are to go by Land upon our parole only one officer to attend us which is a great Indulgance Considering all things Shall not be a Spectacle to the mobbs thro which we shall pass as if we had Guards to attend us I therefore send Diamond back and beg you'll send tomorrow my horse & Chair and a horse for George (the horse I had from Mr Ludlow) You may depend upon my writing to you when ever opertunity Serves upon the road and from Norwich If you should think of any little thing that will be Necessary send it by Diamond Adieu my Dearest Love and may the Great and good God take you my Children & all my Friends into his holy protection and believe me to be with the greatest tenderness & affection your most Affec^t

Husband
FP

Send me Enticks Dictionary
Excuse the Incorrectness of this

A few good Lemons would be verry acceptable by Diamond

My Love to Mr Babcock good M^r & Mrs Shaw and Nancy
Love to all the family & all friends.

4

Horseneck Tues^day 20 Augt 1776

My Dearest Life

We Arrived here yesterday evening and In Company have hired a waggon & 4 horses to transport our baggage to Norwich which will not be Attended with near the Expence we have Agreed with the waggoner to Give him 40^s York per day and to find himself & horses and 20^s per day in return At the rate of 40 miles per Day So that Fowler will be quite unnecessary have therefore Sent him back and Likewise my bedding as that will be useless! I am (thank God) In good Spirits and am in no Anxiety but for you & the Children but my Comfort is I leave you under the protection of a Gracious & Mercifull god who I doubt not will Protect you our Company are all hearty & well and are Just going of Sam Bush was taken into Custody last night for speaking too freely his father is at Fairfield Caution our boy's not to open their lips to any Freinds or foes. My Love to all and am my Dearest Life

Your Affec^te hus^d
FP

5

My Dearest

New Haven Thursday 22^d Aug^t [1776]

I am Just Arrived at This Place after a verry hot & disagreeable Journey tho (thank God) am in Good health and spirits Considering all things and Should be more So was I Assured that that our Seperation did not Affect you So much as I am Confident it must do tho you Pretend to Say to the Contrary but I intreat you not to be dejected on my Acct. As I am Concious that I have done nothing (upon the Strictest Examination) Inimical to the Liberty's of My Country or ever would let the Consequences be what it will nothing affects more then to be taken up in such an hostile manner without any Crime brought to my Charge and without a hearing If this be the Liberty we are Contending for — but I have done And Shall Say no more on that Subject. Tomorrow we Shall Set out for Lebanon the Residence of Governour Trumbull by the way of Middletown, Weathersfield, & Hartford. The wether Continues Extreamly hot which makes it verry disagreable Travilling we can only proceed Early & late which makes but Slow riddance we have been verry Lucky in meeting with Good Entertainment Perticularly good & Clean Lodging to this place our Company is verry Social and Agreeable — Tell good Mr. Babcock that his brother is verry well his father Came here from westerly and attended him untill he was perfectly recovered and is returned home I had not the pleasure to See Mr. Adam Babcock as he is Set out yesterday for Bedford he has it Seems a vessel arrived there from the West India's ladned with Rum & Sugar Just now heard that Mr. Humphry's is made Adjutant of the Militia at Darby and is Gone Down with the Regiment to New York who would thought it I am very positive that I should not have Credited it If a person of veracity had not Informed me of it My Love to sister Morris M^{r.} & Mrs. Shaw the Children M^{r.} & Mrs. Babcock and all friends not forgeting Bet I shall not write any more untill I get to Hartford

Adieu my Dearest and with the Greatest
Sincerely your Affec^{te}
Husband　FP

Excuse this Scraw for I am in ⎫
a room with twenty people ⎬
Speaking all at once. ⎭

Peter Van Schaack:
The Conscience of a Loyalist

William A. Benton

In THE PREFACE to his study *The American Tory,* William Nelson wrote: "The Loyalists in the American Revolution suffered a most abject kind of political failure, losing not only their argument, their war, and their place in American society, but even their proper place in history."[1] As the Bicentennial year approaches, this latter complaint has been, at least to some extent, rectified. In recent years, because of the writing of Nelson, Wallace Brown, Mary Beth Norton, and others, the Loyalists have received more of the attention they deserve.

I believe Nelson was wrong about the abject political failure of at least some of the Loyalists. Several years ago I wrote about a group of men, Whig-Loyalists, who lost their war, but not their argument, and who very rapidly regained their place in society.

During the crisis engendered by the Declaration of Independence, some prominent American Whigs held out and refused to accept independence. To the surprise of the Tories, these men began to come over to the Loyalist camp. One of the most thoughtful and scrupulous of these men was Peter Van Schaack of New York.

Peter Van Schaack was born in Kinderhook, New York, in March 1747, the youngest of seven children. His family was of Dutch origin; his father a moderately well-to-do merchant who served as a magistrate and as a colonel in the militia. Peter entered King's College in 1762, at the age of sixteen. At King's he met and formed lifelong friendships with John Jay, Gouver-

Peter Van Schaack, portrait by an unidentified artist.
(Courtesy New-York Historical Society)

neur Morris, and Robert R. Livingston. He also met and fell in love with Elizabeth Cruger, daughter of the wealthy merchant, Henry Cruger. Much against Mr. Cruger's wishes Peter and Betsy eloped and were married in the autumn of 1765. Peter then proceeded to graduate first in his class from King's College.

Van Schaack decided to become an attorney. With his friend Robert R. Livingston, he studied under William Smith, Jr. Smith described Van Schaack as "the first genius of all the young fellows at New York" in a letter to Philip Schuyler.[2] In January 1769 Peter Van Schaack was licensed to practice before the New York Supreme Court. Soon after he was elected secretary of "The Moot," a legal society in New York City. The legislature later appointed him to collect and revise the statutes of the Province of New York. His revision, covering the period from 1691 to 1773, was published in 1774.[3]

Van Schaack's conduct in the period from 1765 to 1775 was exemplary from the patriot viewpoint. While still in college he wished the "meritorious opposition" to the Stamp Act well.[4] In May 1774 he was elected a member of the Committee of Fifty, formed in New York City to lead the opposition to the Coercive Acts and to serve as a committee of correspondence. Van Schaack, James Duane, and John Jay drew up the rules of the committee.[5]

During this period Van Schaack wrote that American rights and a subordination to Parliament were mutually exclusive. In his words: "Claims so incompatible cannot be reconciled. On one side or other they must be false." He believed that "the benefits arising from our commerce is all Great Britain ought to expect. By grasping at more, they will probably lose all."[6] When the Boston Port Bill was passed he wrote that "an Appeal to the Sword . . . is inevitable." The colonies would never recede from "an absolute Exemption from Parliamentary Taxation in every Respect whatever." This, Van Schaack believed, was their right; and without it they did not "enjoy the Privileges of British subjects. That it *is* their Right is a Conception we cannot expect from England until Necessity should compel them to it."[7]

Peter Van Schaack wanted to go further than the majority of the Committee of Fifty was willing to go at the time. The committee passed a nonimportation agreement. Van Schaack also advocated nonexportation to Britain and the West Indies.[8]

Van Schaack supported the First Continental Congress; and when the Committee of Fifty was dissolved, he was unanimously elected to the Committee of Sixty, which was formed to implement the Continental Association. He was later, in May 1775, appointed to the Committee of Correspondence and Intelligence. At the time he believed that the dispute could not be settled until Britain gave up all powers of taxation. "With respect to Massachusetts Bay: theirs is considered as a *common cause*, and therefore no peace can be established, till the acts relative to them are repealed." To that end, he believed, the recommendations and actions of the Second Continental Congress would "have the force of more than *Law*."[9]

Peter Van Schaack had high hopes for "that great Assembly." As he wrote to one of the New York delegates: "It must be the wish of every good Member of the Community that every Thing might remain Suspended till the Result of your Deliberations are known. . . . Should not private Judgment . . . submit to the united Sense of the collective Body."[10] But his hopes were largely based on a belief that Congress would reject the use of armed force. He did not believe that New York would support the "violent measures" of its neighbors, but would support the Continental Association. "It is a peaceable mode of obtaining redress. It should have a fair trial."[11]

Soon after writing these words Van Schaack moved his family from New York City to his farm at Kinderhook. He suffered from cataracts, and he had trouble reading. His failing eyesight apparently caused his law practice to decline. In addition, his wife and children were ill. He was very solicitous of their health, but two of his children died within a few days of each other in July 1775. Van Schaack's reputation preceded him to

Kinderhook; and soon after his arrival he was elected a member of the Committee of Safety, Correspondence and Protection of Albany County. However, he never became an active member of the committee as his eyesight progressively weakened. By the spring of 1776 he was completely blind in the right eye and had poor vision in the left.[12]

On May 15, 1776, Peter Van Schaack's name was included in a list promulgated by the New York Provincial Congress of persons suspected of having an "equivocal character."[13] On May 29 he was asked to sign a pledge to take up arms against England. Van Schaack refused. He described himself at the time as being among those men who were "disposed to go along with the Congress to a certain limited extent, hoping in that way to fix what they conceived to be the *rights* of their country upon the firmest foundation; but as soon as they found, that the views and designs of the American leaders rested in nothing short of a dissolution of the union between Great Britain and her Colonies, they refused any longer to participate in the public measure."[14]

Here is one clue to the character of Peter Van Schaack. Many of his friends, including John Jay and George Clinton, believed, as Van Schaack did, that the war should be fought for a just place within the British empire. Jay and Clinton acquiesced in the Declaration of Independence, submitting to a *fait accompli*; Peter Van Schaack followed his conscience.

In January 1777 Van Schaack was again called before the committee to take an oath of allegiance to the independent state of New York, again refused, and was exiled to New England. He wandered through Connecticut and Massachusetts with other New York exiles until April when he was allowed to return to Kinderhook through the intercession of John Jay and Governor George Clinton. Van Schaack signed a parole promising to "neither directly or indirectly do or say any thing to the prejudice of the American cause," but at the same time he believed himself to be a British subject.[15] He took this oath to be with his wife, who was quite ill, and believed that it did not violate his principles. As he wrote:

In civil wars, I hold it there can be *no neutrality*; in *mind* I mean. Every man must *wish* one side or the other to prevail. . . . The *ruling powers*, therefore, have a right to consider every person, who does not join them in action, as averse to them in opinions; which will apear the more reasonable, as civil commotions are of such a nature as to give life and activity to the most powerful affections of the human mind.

Have they then a right to *punish* a mere difference of sentiment? By no means. Punishment as such, is due only to overt acts, to the transgression of some known law; and that there may be a strict neutrality *in practice*, is beyond dispute.[16]

Van Schaack maintained this neutral stance until his wife died in the spring of 1778. He then expressed his feelings and allowed himself to be exiled to England, even though it would mean leaving his three surviving children. As he wrote to Theodore Sedgwick, his children had been deprived "of one of the fondest of parents by the visitation of God, and soon to be of another, not indeed for his crimes, nor even indiscretion, but because he dares *think* for himself."[17] Sedgwick had written to Van Schaack pledging his friendship and offering to help care for his children while Van Schaack was in England. Sedgwick also wrote to Aaron Burr, who was to escort Van Schaack to New York City and into exile, to lend Van Schaack any assistance possible, even though Van Schaack "has differed in political opinions from the body of the community in general, and from me in particular."[18]

John Jay also pledged his continuing friendship: "Any services in my power command; I mean never to forget my friends, however different our noses or sentiments may be."[19] Gouverneur Morris also wrote, claiming continued friendship. "I always have regretted . . . that you did not take part with us in the cause. . . . I am particularly afflicted that you should be now obliged to relinquish your country."[20]

I say Van Schaack *allowed* himself to be banished, because Governor George Clinton met Van Schaack in Poughkeepsie

on August 19, 1778, and offered to reverse the act banishing
Van Schaack by treating him as a paroled British prisoner. Van
Schaack refused the offer, but did accept a certificate permit-
ting him to go to England for medical treatment.[21]

Why did Peter Van Schaack, prominent patriot, remain loyal
to Great Britain, and in so doing, give up his home, family,
friends, and position? The answer is to be found first, in his
strong adherence to the principles espoused by John Locke,
particularly those generally referred to under the term "compact theory of government"; second, in his strong sense of
individualism; and third, in his sense of conscience.

His individualism led him to question the unanimity rising
out of the Revolution. He turned inward, and deliberated on
what code of conduct his own conscience would allow him to
follow, for in his words, the consistency of his own conscience
"however insignificant to others, is to me of the utmost impor-
tance."[22]

During the winter of 1775–1776, Peter Van Schaack, on his
Kinderhook farm, re-read and annotated works by Locke,
Vattel, Montesquieu, Grotius, Beccaria, and Pufendorf. He
then wrote a series of reflections on the Revolution in his diary
in January 1776 and expanded on them a year later in a letter to
the Albany Committee of Safety. These deliberations became
his code of conduct.

Van Schaack began by accepting the existence of the Lockean contract. As he put it: "The only foundation of all legitimate
governments, is certainly a compact between the rulers and
the people, containing mutual conditions, and equally obliga-
tory on both the contracting parties." As a natural corollary, the
people had a right to revolt against evil masters, for the doctrine of passive obedience, as expounded by adherents to the
theory of the divine right of kings, was tantamount to slavery.[23]

To Peter Van Schaack the crux of the matter was this question: When was the compact broken, when was the contract
dissolved? Van Schaack believed that without insupportable
tyranny or evil intent the contract could not be dissolved. In
the case at hand, Great Britain and her North American col-

onies, he believed that Britain was misguided, rather than evil. As he wrote: "Taking the whole of the acts complained of together, they do not, I think, manifest a system of slavery, but may fairly be imputed to human frailty and the difficulty of the subject. Many of them seem to have sprung out of particular occasions, and are unconnected with each other. . . . In short, I think these acts may have been passed without a preconcerted plan of enslaving us. . . . I cannot therefore think the government *dissolved*. . . ."[24]

If the government was not dissolved, if the contract had not been broken, then men could not take up arms to overthrow the government, for a state of nature did not exist. As Van Schaack wrote: "As long as the society lasts, the power that every individual gave the society when he entered into it, can never revert to the individual again but will always remain in the community." Van Schaack footnoted these quotations in his diary with one word: "Locke."[25]

Peter Van Schaack realized, he wrote, that many men of principle and integrity had joined the Revolution, including most of his closest friends, but he believed "this is too serious a matter, implicitly to yield to the authority of any character, however respectable. Every man must exercise his own reason, and judge for himself." Van Schaack, following the dictates of his own conscience, believed that the contract had not been dissolved. He wrote that if he were criticized for this stand, as he was, he would ask: "Who has constituted you the judge of the rule of right for me, and what claim have you to infallibility? . . . Do you not differ in opinion as much from me as I do from you, and have I not as much right to blame you as you have me for this difference?"[26]

For the sake of argument, Van Schaack was willing to concede the possibility that the contract had been dissolved in 1776 by the Declaration of Independence "and the British government, as such, totally annihilated here." Then, following Lockean precepts, he wrote, "I conceive that we were reduced to a state of nature, in which the powers of government reverted to the people, who had undoubtedly a right to establish any new form they thought proper." However, since man was "by Nature *free*, *equal* and independent," he regained, upon the dissolution of the contract "That portion of his natural Liberty which each Individual had before surrendered to the Government . . . and to which no one Society could make any Claim until he *incorporated* himself in it."[27]

In claiming that each person could only be released from an allegiance by his own judgment and conscience, Van Schaack brought Locke to bear upon the Revolution in a way the revolutionaries had not considered. When Van Schaack conceded that the contract might have been dissolved in 1776, it followed, according to Locke, that man reverted to a state of nature. The new state governments of the United States could not automatically assume the allegiance of the denizens of the thirteen states. In a state of nature each individual has the right to contract his own new allegiance. He could not be subjected to a new government without his consent. To do so would deprive him of the protection he had under the laws of the old regime, without offering anything in their place except coercion. If the new government, Van Schaack wrote to the Albany Committee of Safety, compelled allegiance or punished those who did not agree with them and would not give up their allegiance to Britain, where were "the sacred rights of mankind" that formed the Revolution's own justification?[28]

For himself, Peter van Schaack believed that he was a citizen of Great Britain. If the contract had not been dissolved, this allegiance was automatic; if it had, he was in a state of nature and entitled to confer his citizenship where he chose. He therefore left New York for exile in England, believing that the United States would achieve independence. With what was perhaps a vision of the future he wrote: "America will perhaps never see such happy days as the past. They may be a great empire, and enjoy opulence; but that mediocrity between extreme poverty and luxurious riches made their condition substantially happy. There being but few offices, there was no scope for bribery, corruption and the numerous train of evils which attend the venality of this country. Henceforth, having an empire of their own, the numerous train of offices will produce like effects as the same causes do here."[29]

Peter Van Schaack arrived in England a loyal subject of the Crown, a man of Lockean principles who believed that the contract had not been dissolved. By 1780 he had changed his mind. From first-hand observation he believed that corruption, dissipation, depravity, and luxury were the dominant features of the British system of government. Britain wanted only, he wrote, "to draw from the colonies a substantial, solid revenue" and had no other interest in their well-being. Van Schaack believed "the British constitution in its most essential principles totally lost," and he therefore found his "mind totally absolved from all ideas of duty." Therefore, the contract having been broken, Peter Van Schaack had reverted to a state of nature and had become "a citizen of the world, and to my native country am I determined to return. . . . Its welfare was the first object of my views, however it may be thought that I had erred in choosing the means to promote it."[30]

By 1783 he considered himself to be "a citizen of the United States, *de jure* at least, whether [he] became so *de facto* or not," and he prepared to return to New York.[31] This statement was made in a letter to John Jay who, in 1784, was able to have the act of attainder against Van Schaack reversed.[32] Van Schaack and Jay had been in contact as early as 1782 when Jay had retained Van Schaack to handle a personal legal matter in England.[33]

Peter Van Schaack landed in New York in July 1785. John Jay met him "like a true Friend. He came on Board the Ship immediately, brought me on Shore, took me to the Governor's, Chief Justice's, etc., and seems determined to do every Thing for me that he can."[34] Van Schaack discovered that his estates and property had never been confiscated, probably because of his ties to many of the leaders of New York's revolutionary efforts. Soon after his return an act of the New York legislature restored his citizenship; he was readmitted to the bar, and opened a law office in Kinderhook.

By 1788 he had regained his prominent position in the

community. He was a Federalist candidate for the New York Ratifying Convention but lost because Columbia County, where Kinderhook is located, was strongly Anti-Federalist. As he wrote: "The popular tide was against us, that is (to be sure) against what was *right* and *good.*" He was then offered, but refused, a Federalist nomination to Congress.[35]

Instead, despite his near blindness, he opened a law school that is considered by the legal historian Paul Hamlin to be the first true law school in the United States.[36] Van Schaack practiced law until 1812 and ran his law school until 1826. In that year Columbia University conferred a Doctor of Laws degree on him. Peter Van Schaack died in September 1832.

Peter Van Schaack was somewhat unusual among Loyalists, not only in his return to the United States, but also because he did not decline into insignificance as American independence was gained. The Hutchinsons, the Olivers, the DeLanceys, the Galloways, never regained any significant measure of political influence. But Peter Van Schaack and other Whig-Loyalists did, some in the independent United States, others in the British empire. To name a few, William Smith, Jr., under whom Van Schaack had studied law, became Chief Justice of Quebec; Daniel Leonard of Massachusetts became Chief Justice of Bermuda; Andrew Allen of Philadelphia became a prominent barrister in England; and perhaps most significant, William Samuel Johnson of Connecticut became a United States Senator and first president of Columbia College.

Why did Peter Van Schaack and these others have such a relatively easy time regaining their positions in society? I think it likely that, because they were revolutionaries and patriots before the Declaration of Independence, they were part of the mainstream of American political thought. They shared a common political philosophy with the revolutionaries. After independence was declared Van Schaack and the others supported the British Crown because of a political philosophy that was essentially Lockean and Whiggish. The Whig-Loyalists differed from the patriots only over the question of independence. Van Schaack and the others did not object to the general trend taken by the Revolution. Therefore it was a relatively simple matter for Peter Van Schaack, once he had accepted independence, to throw himself wholeheartedly into the life of the new nation.

William Franklin:
The Making of a Conservative

Willard S. Randall

E VER SINCE a self-serving colonial official characterized New Jersey inhabitants as "the most Easie and happy people of any collony in America,"[1] numerous history writers have been content to hand down a simplistic image of "the garden of America" and its supposedly soporific state in the complicated era ending in independence. The scenario painted by these historians depicts frugal, uneducated farmers contentedly following their fat oxen through sandy furrows, occasionally carting themselves off to the province's sleepy twin capitals of Burlington and Perth Amboy to tend to a minimum of government chores, paying little or no taxes and even less heed to the nettlesome events beyond their windrows until two contesting armies unexpectedly materialized to trample down the turnips.[2]

Even a preliminary glimpse at colonial politics must show some weeds in the garden, especially if the focus is tightened to the regime of William Franklin, longest in office and last in line to wrestle with the divided colony's stubborn problems and even more stubborn constituents.[3]

What distinguishes New Jersey's prewar experience from those of other, more dramatically portrayed, colonies is the strong influence of persistent local issues and personalities and the unique political responses of the long-tenured Franklin, who very nearly brought off a separate peace with England that very well might have broken the "rope of Sand" of continental union and aborted the revolution.[4]

56

William Franklin, portrait attributed to Mather Brown. (Courtesy Mrs. J. Manderson Castle, Jr. and the Frick Art Reference Library)

Certainly little of this seemed imminent when a gay cavalcade of sleigh-riding aristocrats and handsomely mounted Middlesex County horseguards rode out on the icy morning of February 25, 1762, to welcome William Franklin and his bride Elizabeth into the eastern capital of Perth Amboy.[5] Indeed, as the townspeople managed a shivering welcome, there was little even to hint that Franklin, a thirty-two-year-old career politician from Philadelphia, would remain in the Jerseys any longer than it had taken many of his predecessors to find more lucrative posts elsewhere in His Majesty's service.[6]

Actually, there was little to hold an ambitious young man such as Franklin. Groomed to the politest literary and social circles of Philadelphia and London despite his bastardy, already he had served as clerk to the Pennsylvania Assembly and comptroller of the Philadelphia post office (both posts procured by his father's powerful patronage), and for his part in his father's famous scientific experiments he had been honored by Oxford University with a Master of Arts degree. On his own merits, moreover, he had trained in Pennsylvania and New Jersey law under the brilliant tutelage of young Joseph Galloway before serving the customary term at the Middle Temple that led to being called to the London bar.

A dashing young man "with the eye and figure of a veteran," he carried himself with the distinction gained as a youthful captain at Fort Ticonderoga in the third French and Indian War. A founder of the American Society for Promoting and Propagating Useful Knowledge in Philadelphia, and an initiator of that city's elite Assembly, he had mingled with the leaders of America's and Britain's highest circles of art, science, and politics.[7]

If he planned a career of administering to New Jersey's populace of 70,000, there was enough to engage his energies. After sixty years of royal rule that had done little more than unite the Jerseys on paper, there still was no governor's residence, no permanent government buildings, no acceptable boundary line, few good roads and bridges, no thriving seaport, only one incipient college.[8] Worse still, from young

Franklin's standpoint, winter and summer the governor was obliged to curry favor among pennypinching legislators to have his salary renewed, hopefully at no decrease, for it was cynically assumed he would find some device for enhancing his meager allowance.[9]

If he succeeded in keeping the delicate peace among liberal western Quakers, conservative eastern gentry, and thousands of riot-prone Scotch-Irish squatters, if he somehow followed the time-lapsed, unsympathetic, yet dreadfully precise instructions of the remote Commissioners of Trade in London, he could expect, in a reasonable number of years, advancement out of the colony; if not, as was the case with his immediate predecessor Josiah Hardy, disgrace and dismissal.[10]

Nevertheless, the post *was* coveted, and its dashing new incumbent had won it after making a striking impression in Britain, where the Earl of Bute, current favorite of the King and Queen Mother, had personally recommended him, evidently without the direct influence of the elder Franklin, to the Earl of Halifax, head of the Board of Trade, who seemed satisfied, after an exhaustive, unprecedented personal interrogation of the candidate.[11]

At first it appeared young Franklin faced the additional handicap of his shadowy birth as illegitimate, if acknowledged son of well-known Dr. Franklin. "It is no less amazing than true," wrote irate Pennsylvania proprietor John Penn to his friend, William Alexander, Lord Stirling, "If any *gentleman* had been appointed it would have been a different case . . . I make no doubt but the people of New Jersey will make some remonstrance upon this indignity put upon them."[12]

Doubtless, Penn had more to concern him than pedigree. The younger Franklin, his confederate Galloway, and Dr. Franklin had long been the Whiggish scourges of Pennsylvania proprietors. This new appointment, managed so quietly and skillfully in England portended an even more powerful trans-Delaware alliance. In fact, the elder Franklin had taken his son to London five years earlier to convince the court that Pennsylvania should follow New Jersey in its conversion from proprietorship to Crown colony, even as Galloway kept up pressure at home in the Pennsylvania Assembly to tax proprietary lands equally with all others. It was not too great a leap for the Penn faction to imagine that one Franklin coveted the far more powerful post of first royal governor of Pennsylvania while the other ruled across the river.[13]

If the legislators assembling in Burlington in May 1763 shared this concern or objected to the bar sinister on the new governor's coat-of-arms, they had a strange way of showing it, increasing his salary a healthy £200 and voting him a housing allowance. Apparently many were pleased with his good sense in passing up the proffered invitation to Perth Amboy to dwell in the nearly completed proprietary palace, symbol of faction between rural voters and land-rich proprietors.[14]

Instead, he chose the bustling rivertown of Burlington, seat of Quaker dominance[15] only seventeen miles upriver from his familial and social power base at Philadelphia. At Burlington, he began buying up real estate, built a handsome three-story brick mansion of his own, where he could sit on the columned porch, look out over the broad lawns to the sycamore-lined river, and ponder the persistent problems that must plague him like every other governor in the colony's history: insufficient currency, almost no foreign exchange, simmering feuds over land titles, no way to pay official salaries without, from his viewpoint, grovelling before the Assembly.[16] From his veranda, he could see a possible solution to this last problem: In the Delaware River were unclaimed islands with rich farmland. It occurred to him that this land might be annexed by the Crown, rented back to farmers, and the income thus realized earmarked to pay official salaries. He communicated this scheme to London at once.[17]

While there was no guarantee that the Assembly would abide such a barefaced grab for its power over the pursestrings, guaranteed by the Concessions and Agreements of 1664, it was nevertheless ominous for Franklin that the Commissioners of Trade in London ignored the request and left Franklin's administration at the mercy of the Assembly. Without support

from London on this key issue, it would be virtually impossible
for him to untangle the colony's festering fiscal problems,
which quickly multiplied as the era of postwar economic decline set in.[18]

While New Jersey had minor casualties at the hands of
marauding Indians along its exposed northwest frontier, it had
gained great dividends in the war. Great Britain poured in
troops who freely spent hard money. Parliament paid subsidies
to the Jerseymen that were applied, in an early example of
revenue-sharing, to eliminate provincial taxes. The hungry
war machine exchanged hard coin-of-the-realm for hemp;
black oak and pine for shipbuilding; wheat, corn, and cotton;
barrel hoops and staves; anything that could assist in the
worldwide struggle.

In a temporary lapse of mercantilism and the royal prerogative, the Assembly was allowed to issue vast amounts of paper
money, which debt-ridden colonists shrewdly sent to creditors
in England to retire long-standing accounts. But the boom
swung back at war's end, the artificial prosperity deflated, and
the second-smallest populace in any colony in America woke
up saddled with a £300,000 debt, highest in America. While
the American colonial debt averaged 18 shillings, in New
Jersey it amounted to £15 for every male between eighteen and
sixty, rivalling the £18 burden in England![19]

As the depression deepened, Parliament seized the moment
to reassert its right to regulate colonial currency, in February
1764 outlawing paper money as legal tender,[20] and also to the
absolute power of taxation, serving notice in August of its
intent to impose a stamp tax—similar to England's—on all
newspapers and legal instruments to help defray the £350,000
cost of maintaining a 10,000-man garrison in America. Jerseymen groaned at the news.[21]

Governor Franklin, busily proposing and winning London's
approval of trade-nourishing bounties on hemp, flax, and silk,
as part of an unprecedented legislative package of 35 bills,
apparently was no less surprised at the swift reaction than most
Americans.[22]

One trained observer, Woodbridge printer James Parker (erstwhile New York partner of Benjamin Franklin), shortly before he issued a wildly revolutionary blast at Parliament, coolly took the measure of the move in a letter to Attorney-General Cortlandt Skinner:

> There is such a general scarcity of Cash that nothing we have will Command it and Real Estates of Every kind are falling at least one-half in Value. Debtors that were a year or two ago responsible for £1000 can not now Raise a fourth part of the sum. . . . there is an Entire Stop to all sales by the sheriffs for want of Buyers, and Men of the best Estates amongst us can scarce Raise money enough to defray the Necessary Expences of their families. . . . Under the Insupportable Distress We are now called upon for many thousands of pounds Sterling to be paid by a Stamp Duty. . .[23]

Parker, who was also secretary of the postal service in America, issued the first revolutionary newspaper on September 21, 1765; the single-issue *Constitutional Courant*, distributed on the streets of New York City and along country roads by post riders, was quickly suppressed.[24]

Again setting the pattern for other colonies, New Jersey's lawyers met September 19, 1765, in Perth Amboy and agreed to conduct no business requiring the obnoxious stamps, which meant no business at all. When they met again on February 23, 1766, many were suffering hardships from their resolve, and all were under pressure from the presence of 800 Sons of Liberty who had marshalled in case the lawyers wavered. The lawyers voted to suspend business until April 1, when, if the law was not repealed, they would break it and resume practice without using stamps, giving in to the wishes of the radicals.[25]

All over New Jersey, there were protests. When the stamps arrived off New York on the *Royal Charlotte*, Franklin, on the advice of William Alexander, refused to let them be landed, saying there was no safe place on the entire coast. The stamp commissioner, William Coxe, had resigned before the law took effect, forfeiting a £3,000 bond, when he was refused the rental of a house unless he could guarantee it would not be pulled to pieces by the mob. To make sure he did not reconsider, the New Brunswick Sons of Liberty followed him to Philadelphia, coercing him into taking an oath not to handle the stamps.

Pleading that he had no clear instructions from London, Governor Franklin exhibited uncommon shrewdness and skill during the crisis. When there was no collector for stamps and no armed place in New Jersey to protect them, he arranged to have a British troop contingent on alert in New York, then had the stamps transferred to *H.M.S. Sardoine,* anchored in the harbor off Perth Amboy. When the captain asserted that he had to put the ship into drydock and strip it of its guns for the winter, Governor Franklin stalled, appealing to Lt. Gov. Cadwallader Colden of New York for permission to store the stamps at Fort George. Colden replied that that would be impossible because the fort was filled with troops and supplies; there simply was no room!

Turning to the Navy again, he convinced the *Sardoine's* captain to take the stamps wherever he planned to keep his ship's stores for the winter, reasoning shrewdly that the citizens of one colony would not attack the stamps of another.

Despite his efforts at discouraging the Assembly, the legislators met at Sproul's Tavern in Perth Amboy after the House was dissolved and voted belatedly to send delegates to a continental Stamp Congress in New York. When New Jersey Speaker Robert Ogden refused to sign the resulting petition to the King, he was burned in effigy all over New Jersey, and felt obliged to resign promptly from public life.[26]

At this time, Franklin's long involvement in Philadelphia politics bore bitter fruit. The Proprietary Party, accusing the Franklins of fostering the Stamp Act—and William in particular of trying to block the New Jersey delegates from attending the New York Congress—publicly libelled him. Forced to issue broadsides throughout the city, he hurried to the Franklin home in Philadelphia, where his mother Deborah and sister Sarah had armed and barricaded themselves along with friends, against the menacing mobs.

By now, Franklin, thoroughly shaken, appealed to the public press; his absolute denial of the easily disproven lies about his involvement swung the mob's wrath away from him; and fortunately word reached Philadelphia of his father's brilliant defense of American rights before the House of Commons. Young Franklin, somewhat aged by the affair, admitted he had feared his house would be "pulled down about my ears and all my Effects destroyed."[27] When news of repeal reached Burlington, the governor and his lady joined the public celebration, firing off two small cannons on his lawn and joining in eighteen toasts, to everyone's obvious relief.[28]

That young Franklin was sympathetic to the Whig-American cause, that he referred to "the people" while other Crown officials deplored "the mob," that he openly refused to support the hated Customs Service as the stamp crisis was followed by the Townshend crisis and a burgeoning smuggling industry in Cape May, Delaware Bay, and Little Egg Harbor Inlet, all seem to dispute the long-held theory that he had, by this time, long since "turned Tory" to get and hold his governor's chair.[29]

What seems more the case is that Jerseymen were startled to find they had a successful, shrewd governor who was not afraid to compromise to uphold the Crown's prerogative, and, as the informed man on the scene, to use his good judgment to advance the welfare of the colony.

In this regard, Franklin often had to bully the bullheaded Assembly. While he seems to have despaired of wringing a higher salary and living allowance from the legislators and dropped his plans for a suitable official residence in the face of widespread economic dislocation, he pushed vigorously for badly needed reforms.

His welfare plan to feed and clothe destitute Sussex and Monmouth County farmers, his support of the Anglican Church's retired clergy, his espousal of a second college in the colony, his campaign for more and better roads and bridges built with proceeds of public lotteries, and most of all, his

successful eleven-year battle for a loan-office to alleviate the
cash shortage and to self-liquidate government operational
expenses all were visionary pieces of liberal legislation years
ahead of their time.[30] And while each excited the wrath of
various factions, they combined to free him for a grander
scheme.

When the British, by the Proclamation of 1763, took over
the huge wedge of real estate bordered by the Ohio and
Mississippi Rivers and the Appalachian Mountain chain, the
land was reserved as an Indian reservation under Crown protection. But part of the plan was to drive off thousands of
squatters and subsequently to sell the land and provide a large
source of quit-rents to reduce the national debt and defray
costs of the royal military establishment.[31]

The Franklins, father and son, along with leading Quaker
merchants in Philadelphia and Indian agents in New York,
grasped the possibility of creating new provinces, one of which
was to be called Vandalia, and would consist of much of
present-day Indiana and Illinois. To promote the development
of this colony, Governor Franklin, who as a young man had
explored the territory with Conrad Weiser, set up communications between Sir William Johnson and George Croghan, his
assistant in New York, and the wealthy Whartons of Philadelphia.[32]

It was crucial to keep friendly relations with the Indians
inhabiting the lands, and the Franklins surreptitiously pursued
this end with pen and sword, leading the unpopular protest
against the Paxton Boys' massacre of Christianized Conestoga
Indians in Lancaster County, Pennsylvania, and the similar
killing of peaceful Indians in northwestern New Jersey. Their
plan was bold, costing the elder Franklin a loss of his Assembly
seat in the bitter 1764 election and permanently antagonizing
frontier Jerseymen against William Franklin when he insisted
on hanging the murderers of Indians.

Meanwhile, Governor Franklin expanded his real estate
holdings, buying up valuable lands in New York and New
Jersey. Acquiring 575 acres of choice riverfront in Burlington

county, he turned Franklin Park into a showcase scientific farm, where he conducted many experiments in husbandry, tilling, and breeding that he evidently intended to practice on a grander scale farther west.[33]

That he was sure the great scheme would ultimately succeed is apparent from his outspoken stands before the Assembly which he accused of neglecting the public welfare by ignoring his programs of public works and crop bounties[34] and by his long, hot reply when Lord Hillsborough wrongly accused him of neglecting his duty and allowing a Massachusetts circular letter to be read before the Assembly.[35]

As Edgar J. Fisher sagely observed, "Gov. Franklin's endeavors for the prosperity and welfare of the province were earnest and unremitting . . . had Franklin been governor of New Jersey a decade earlier, there is no reason to doubt that his administration would have been far more successful than it was."[36]

After a decade of push and tug, Governor Franklin and the Assembly finally parted company in 1773 over the theft of the tax returns of East Jersey from the home of Treasurer Stephen Skinner. Although Franklin had the Samuel Ford gang hunted down and two of its members confessed the theft of £7,854 from Skinner's house, the Assembly, insisting that the wealthy Perth Amboy aristocrat had been negligent, refused to investigate further, demanded restitution from Skinner, and his resignation. Franklin, angrily protesting this incursion on the royal prerogative, doggedly held on for five months until Skinner finally resigned.[37]

This public furor masked a deeper malaise, however, brought on by the increasing frequency of mob violence centering in Essex County. Many of its residents were transplanted New Englanders with radical views who for nearly thirty years had intermittently rioted against the proprietors, mobbed crown officials, and kept their leaders out of jail.[38]

Governor Franklin saw the storm clouds gathering. By now the Vandalia charter seemed a distant dream, as Hillsborough and his friends in London went out of their way to destroy the

Franklins. The younger Franklin came under suspicion in London, was passed over for preferment, was denied the governorship of Barbadoes, birthplace of his ailing wife.[39]

Late in 1773, Governor Franklin, angered that his father's politics had damaged him, irritated that his father thought him so subservient, took a bold step. Placing Franklin Park and his Burlington mansion on the market, he moved the seat of government to Perth Amboy, where he could be near his few close friends on the Council in the growing crisis.

His move to the magnificent Proprietary House—with its marble floors, rich panelling, deer park, orchards, lake, and stables for twelve carriage horses seems to have severed him as much as his loyalty to the Perth Amboy aristocracy had from Whig affections, bringing him finally within the orbit of the very Tories who had once spurned this bastard but now sought the comfort and protection of his official presence.[40]

But by now his enemies were many, powerful, and determined to bring him down. His sponsorship of Rev. Jonathan Odell, pastor of St. Mary's Anglican Church in Burlington, where he and his wife had been active parishioners, provoked the anger of the Presbyterians, who thought they smelled a popish plot to create an American bishopric at Burlington.[41]

Using Governor Franklin's friendship,[42] Richard Stockton had travelled to Scotland and persuaded the firebrand Rev. John Witherspoon to migrate to Princeton and lead the disestablishment drive to repel the Anglicans and their supporters.[43]

Joining their ranks was rich and influential William Livingston, who since Yale College days had been preaching the evils of Anglican episcopacy. In 1770, he moved his estate and law practice to Liberty Hall in Elizabethtown, Essex County.[44]

Sickened by the growing dissension, Governor Franklin, soon after hearing of his father's disgrace before the Privy Council in the Whately affair, urged him to come home. They had drifted apart ideologically over the years; the son, the younger Franklin, remaining the more moderate; the father, the elder Franklin, deciding by 1774 that:

Parliament has no right to make any law whatever binding on
the Colonies. . . . I know your sentiments differ from mine
on these subjects. You are a thorough government man,
which I do not wonder at, nor do I aim at converting you. I
only wish you to act uprightly and steadily, avoiding that
duplicity which . . . adds contempt to indignation. If you can
promote the prosperity of your people and leave them hap-
pier than you found them, whatever your political principles
are, your memory will be honored.[45]

While it was evident that the two Franklins had parted
politically, the son feared for the safety of his father, writing to
him December 24, 1774, informing him of the death of Benjamin's wife, pleading with him to come home:

If there was any Prospect of your being able to bring the
People in power to your way of thinking, or of those of your
way of thinking being brought into power, I should not think
so much of your stay. But as you have had pretty strong
proofs that neither can be reasonably expected and that you
are looked upon with an Evil Eye in that Country, you had
certainly better return. . .

By September 1774 as the First Continental Congress as-
sembled at Philadephia to protest the closing of the Boston
port, Governor Franklin and his good friend Galloway had
decided, after long discussions that summer, that what would
make his people happiest would be peace, and if his father had
abandoned hope for reconciliation, the younger men must
make the effort.[46]

Modifying the plan of union the elder Franklin had advanced
in Albany twenty years earlier, Galloway argued passionately
for a continental legislature co-equal with Parliament, with a
Supreme Executive appointed by the King. The plan, tabled
by Congress by a narrow 6 to 5 vote after a last-ditch attack by
the New England democrats who bitterly opposed an Anglo-
American commonwealth, was praised in New York and Lon-

don after it was anxiously forwarded to Lord Dartmouth in England.[47]

As the determined Sons of Liberty enforced nonimportation in New Jersey, as protest and recruitment flourished, events now swept past Governor Franklin, leaving this erstwhile Whig moderate a dogged conservative in their wake. In January 1775 even before the bloodletting at Lexington-Concord, he gravely addressed the Assembly:

> It is not for me to decide on the particular Merits of the Dispute between Great Britain and her colonies, nor do I mean to censure those who conceive themselves aggrieved, for aiming at a Redress of the Grievances. It is a Duty they owe themselves, their Country, and their Posterity. All that I could wish to guard you against is the giving any Countenance or Encouragement to that destructive mode of Proceeding. . . . You have now pointed out to you, Gentlemen, two Roads, one evidently leading to Peace, Happiness, and a Restoration of the Public Tranquility—the other inevitably conducting you to Anarchy, Misery, and all the Horrors of a Civil War."[48]

This sober appeal served to suspend New Jersey in the eye of the hurricane for many months, until news thundered south over the old Post Road that farmers and redcoats had clashed bloodily outside Boston. Everywhere, instantly, militia met, marched, drilled; citizens associated, swore oaths, and enforced them, seizing and disarming recalcitrant Tories, purging them from their ranks.[49]

In a bitter falling-out, Governor Franklin purged Lord Stirling from his Council for accepting a militia command. Stirling, raiding British commerce, intercepted Franklin's "secret and Confidential" official correspondence to London, and with the acquiescence of Congress, ordered a guard placed on the governor's palace at 2 A.M. on January 8, 1776.[50]

A month later, many Jerseymen were still undecided: Elias Boudinot, shocked by Rev. Witherspoon's incendiary 90-

minute harangue for independence at a secret caucus of the
Committees of Correspondence at Woodbridge, "was at my
wit's end, to know how to extricate myself from so disagreeable
a situation . . . two or three Gent' [sic] of the Audience came to
me and desired that I would inform the Doctor, that if he
proceeded any farther they would not be answerable for his
safety . . . out of 36 Members, there were but 3 or 4 who Voted
for the Doctor's proposition, the rest rejecting it with great
warmth."[51]

In this climate, Franklin prevailed on the Assembly to in-
struct its delegates to Congress against independence and
instead to petition legally through him to the King for redress
of grievances. The Assembly agreed. Alarmed, Congress sent
three delegates to Burlington to argue against a separate peace.
The Assembly wavered, fell into line—"not wanting to appear
singular" and an angry Franklin refused to forward their petition.[52]

On receiving a special message of King and Parliament
offering limited grounds for negotiation, Franklin, now the last
hope of conciliation, summoned the Assembly to meet on June
10. The New Jersey Provincial Congress, in urgent session,
decided that this was in direct contempt of a Continental
Congress resolution "that it is necessary that every kind of
government under the Crown, should be suppressed." The
Provincial Congress ruled that the governor had "acted in
direct contempt and violation of the resolve of the Continental
Congress," and ordered his arrest.[53]

For months, the courageous Franklin had stayed on in the
face of personal danger, long after other royal officials had fled.
His gallant stand, which he justified by saying he would not
give Congress the excuse of creating a government because he
had left none, masked his fear. In a letter to Lord Dartmouth in
September 1775 he wrote, "It would mortify me extremely to
be seized upon and led like a Bear through the Country to some
Place of Confinement in New England."[54]

Only a month after he was taken in June 1776 from his ailing
wife—who would flee to New York and die there without

ARREST OF WILLIAM FRANKLIN BY ORDER OF CONGRESS
The Last Royal Governor of New Jersey, Son of Benjamin Franklin

"The Arrest of William Franklin," a contemporary print
from the magazine *Specimen Illustration*. (Courtesy New
Jersey Historical Society)

seeing him again—only one month later the great British fleet would arrive off Perth Amboy and the Governor's father would come to Perth Amboy to negotiate with the British peace commissioners. There is room to speculate what a difference the presence of both Franklins would have made at the parley, for which Governor Franklin had held out so bravely, so long.[55]

By then, however, he had been tried by a court he refused to recognize, insulted by its president, Rev. Witherspoon, because of his "exalted birth," and guarded so closely he sometimes could not "answer nature's call,"[56] then led off, as he had dreaded, to Connecticut and a succession of ever-worsening prisons until, in his own words, he was released from the subterranean dungeons of Simsbury Mines "considerably reduced in flesh" and exchanged two years later.[57]

Before the long war ended, Governor Franklin would stand accused of authorizing, as president of the Board of Associated Loyalists, the brutal retaliatory hanging of a rebel officer. In the ensuing furor, he was never allowed to testify, was bundled off to Britain ostensibly to plead the Loyalist cause.[58]

But the bitterest hour had already passed, as his wife lay dying and a vindictive Congress refused him a pass to see her one last time. Certainly it would only have taken a word from his father to see that his only son received mercy should he ever need it. But the father would never forgive the son, would do all he could to chastise all Loyalists at the signing of the peace treaty, would go to *his* grave denouncing William in his will. It was ironic that William, who had much more to forgive, would try to heal the open wounds in his shattered family, would go to *his* grave in London in exile in 1813, writing of his dream, of the new land his father and his friends had dreamed of long ago.

For William Franklin had ever been the visionary of the two, dreaming of a great Anglo-American empire where men could live in peace and prosperity, where English earls and Indians and self-made Americans could sustain each other with the fruit and toils of their incredibly vast domains.

And when the dream had wavered, when the march of events had passed him by, he could not bring himself to desert his post, to break faith with the oaths he had given his King and the promises he had made to himself, his family, and his country.

A century later, he would have been acclaimed as a symbol of the sterling qualities of British loyalty and leadership. But in the bitter family quarrel of 1776, he was a man mistrusted, misunderstood, and maligned by both sides.

The New York Loyalists:
A Cross-section of Colonial Society

Esmond Wright

THE SIGNIFICANCE of New York Loyalists in the Revolution is a subject to approach with caution, even with trepidation. For New Yorkers, and much more for Englishmen, it is a subject charged with historical and political emotion. Indeed, it was once charged with risk. When "God Save The King" was sung at a Loyalist party in Mayor Abraham Cuyler's home in Albany on June 4, 1776, an outraged citizenry broke in and carried the singers off to jail.

Even after the war, passions died slowly. When Washington Irving's legendary Rip Van Winkle came down from his mountain, his eyesight failing and his beard long and white, he found a crowd before the village inn, but it was a different inn from the one he had known. The sign that swung there did not seem to portray the familiar ruby face of King George, but rather a man in a blue and buff coat, under whose portrait was lettered "General Washington." When the crowd demanded to know who he was, and what he was doing there, he quavered, "I am a poor quiet man, a native of this place, and a loyal subject to the King, God bless him! . . . Here a general shout burst from the bystanders—'A tory! a tory! a spy! a refugee! hustle him! away with him!'"

Moreover, Loyalist history is unusual, in that it is not the story of success, but of failure. G. K. Chesterton once described historians as perpetual snobs, since it was their function to justify and explain success. Historians of the Loyalists hardly meet that criterion, since they chronicle reiterated

74

A contemporary British cartoonist's view of the treatment of
Loyalists. (Courtesy Library of Congress)

injuries, usurpations, and hardships. It can, of course, be contended that present-day Canada is a political success story, partly because it is a product of the Loyalist settlers' qualities of endurance and stoicism. In lesser measure, the story of some West Indian Islands, which had infusions of Loyalism before and after 1783, is similar. But for the most part the Loyalist story is one of human suffering and tragedy. Loyalism is over-whelmingly a story of people who lost all—a war, their lands, their status in society, and their place in the world. And the America that was left behind, the Whig world that, in Louis Hartz's phrase, "inherited democracy without having to fight for it," was a totally different world from that which might have been the Anglo-American Atlantic community.

The Anglo-American world was not just the dream of William Franklin, but of his father, Benjamin Franklin, the "Old England" man of the 1760s who was, like the great majority, a most reluctant revolutionary. He saw the storm clouds very late. Yet he was also a modern-minded man of remarkable vision. He advocated the moving of the court to, and the siting of the capital in, the New World. He foresaw that the growth of American manufacturing could make that New World a totally transformed Anglo-American world. It was not just Ben Franklin's vision, but that of all of the Anglo-Americans, perhaps the majority, who guessed wrong.

The Loyalist story offers a comparison with that other great traumatic experience in American history, the Civil War. Loyalism and the Old South each had common features: lead-ership by an established elite, a sense of noblesse oblige, a preoccupation with rural virtues and with order and hierarchy in society, a difficulty in accepting, and adapting to, change, and in the end a readiness to go to war. But the Loyalists, for the most part, went into exile and died on alien shores. The Southerners stayed on to suffer and endure.

An historical assessment of the Loyalists must begin with the Audit Office Papers, Series 12 and 13. The first series, in 146 volumes, contains the claims; and the second, in 141 volumes, is the evidence submitted by the Loyalists in support of their

claims.[1] In all, 5,072 claims were put before the British Commissioner from 1782 to 1789; 954 were withdrawn or not followed through; and 4,118 were examined, of which 1,401 were
from claimants who were by that time in Canada. The total
amount of money claimed by "the American Sufferers" was
£8,026,045. The Commissioners noted the total in April 1790
as £10,358,413.39. The amount allowed, says Wallace Brown,
came to £3,292,452; the Commissioners said £3,033,091.2.11.
The discrepancies may well be due to the pensions and doles
paid before the 1782 investigation began.

The most valuable analysis of these claims has been made by
Professor Wallace Brown of the University of New Brunswick,
in two studies, *The King's Friends*, a heavily statistical break-
down of the Loyalists state by state (and in itself an elaboration
of his Ph.D dissertation at the University of California), and in
his book, *The Good Americans*.[2] His analysis has been
criticized by Eugene Fingerhut in the *William and Mary Quarterly*, who charged that the claimants did not necessarily con-
stitute a representative sample of all the Loyalists:

Thus, several important qualifications must be considered if
the Loyalist claims are to be studied quantitatively. The
petitioners with several occupations may have had as many
economic interests. Many of those who took the British side
did not emigrate, and most of the emigrants were not claimants. The petitioners' homes were not distributed throughout the colonies in the same manner as were all loyalist
residences. Inflated currencies, collusion among petitioners, and fraud, raise many claims above their true values. On
the other hand, missing legal proofs of ownership, the commission's regulations on property possessed, and requests
merely for lost salaries probably caused some understate-
ments. In addition, the graphic representations of the claims
indicate that their values are grouped in an unexpected
pattern. Further complications could result, moreover,
when two distortions occurred in the same claim. For example, the conversion of currency to sterling probably inflated

values, but omission of property from the claim reduced the number of items presented to the commission. Therefore, since the emigrants are not a statistically valid sample of the loyalists, since the claimants are not representative of the emigrants, and since the transcripts do not present accurate quantitative data about the claimants' possessions, one may seriously question a statistical use of this source to describe beyond what compensation or pensions the petitioners sought.[3]

These comments are valid ones. Also, the great majority of the Loyalists would naturally be passive and would not seek, after 1783, to reveal their former loyalism, Many were remote from or ignorant of the commission. Nevertheless, the 5,000 claims are significant, useful, and thoroughly documented. Any comment on the Loyalists must surely be based primarily on this substantial evidence in the Audit Office Papers, supported by the Colonial Offiice, Series 5.[4]

There were 1,107 claims from New York State, that is, almost 25 percent of those who might be called "authentic" claimants were New Yorkers, although in population size the state was only seventh out of thirteen. These claimants constituted 0.5 percent of the population of the state, which was then estimated to be 203,000, i.e., one in two hundred. Indeed, the claims from New York City itself constituted 13 percent of all the claims, and approximately 0.5 percent of *its* population (estimated at 25,000). All the claimants were strongly urban. Of the Pennsylvanian claimants, half lived in Philadephia; 60 percent of the Maryland claimants came from Annapolis and Baltimore.

New York was in fact the most loyal of all the colonies, both relative to the others and in sheer numbers. This statistical evidence is confirmed by the contemporary references. Both John Adams and Alexander Hamilton said that in 1776 half the population of New York was Tory. The British ex-Loyalist physician turned diplomat, Phineas Bond, said that in the end 100,000 Loyalists were exiled; and it is likely that there were perhaps three or four times that number who were, in their hearts, loyal but who stayed neutral. A detailed piece of work on this point is Paul Smith's article in the *William and Mary Quarterly*,[5] in which he concluded that the Loyalists equaled 16 percent of the population, i.e., 500,000, or 1 in 6 of the total population. Wilbur Siebert's estimate for New York exiles in London is 6,000.[6] Alexander Flick in his study of New York Loyalists, published in 1901, came to a similar conclusion; the Loyalists, he says, numbered 90,000 out of 203,000; and of these, 35,000 emigrated.[7]

Moreover, New York was loyal in the real sense of the word; it put its men into action. Two out of three of the New York claimants claimed to have served in the Armed Forces, which in the eyes of the investigating commission was the arch-test of loyalty. New York provided 23,500 men for the British Armed Forces, and it is unlikely that the total American contribution to such regular forces was more than 50,000 in all. "No colony," says Wallace Brown, "contributed more to British military power." Among the prestige units put into the field were the New York Loyalists (DeLancey's Brigade, the Westchester Refugees); the King's Royal Regiment of New York or "Johnson's Greens" (for which Sir John Johnson received a commission in June 1776); the King's Orange Rangers (John Bayard's); the Guides and Pioneers; the Loyal American Regiment (Robinson's Regiment); the King's Rangers; Richard Rogers' The Queen's Rangers; the King's American Regiment (Edmund Fanning's); the Prince of Wales American Regiment (Montforte Browne's); and Jessup's Corps. These New York regiments, plus those from Nova Scotia and Canada, probably constituted a half or more of all Loyalists in arms during the war; and the early establishment of these forces may well have been responsible for Germain's belief in ever-flowing Loyalist military support. It was to prove oversanguine.

One must distinguish between the Loyalism of New York City and that of the State. The situation of New York City in the American Revolution was, of course, unique. But then New York City is, and always has been, a unique place. Did it not in the Civil War seriously contemplate secession from the North in order to trade with both sides? Thomas Chandler recommended precisely this move in 1776. As a city, living by trade and commerce, its prerequisite was peace. When John Adams spoke of revolutionary America as being one third Whig, one third Tory and one third mongrel, did he have New York City in mind for his third category? But in fact this figure would be too high.

New York City's Loyalism was simply a consequence of its location. It was the natural base for any campaign to cut off New England from the Middle Colonies. As the major British military stronghold throughout the seven years of war, it became in fact a Fortress Britannica, part refuge, part port, and part supply base for the British Army, dependent on its stormy and vulnerable Atlantic line of communication. There had never been much affection shown by the Patriots for those who lived by trade in the seaports or in the Tidewater. Too many of them were Scots, most of whom proved to be Tories, and almost all of whom were unpopular; even their accents were unwelcome. The Scots were mainly factors at the ports, or Highland Catholic tenants of Sir William Johnson in the Mohawk Valley, or, in North Carolina, recent arrivals in the rebellious back-country where the Regulator movement was strong. They were all strikingly loyal to the flag, but very unpopular.

To these sources of Loyalism in New York City, the presence of a large British and German Army was an additional spur to trade and commerce. Troops had to be accommodated, and the homes of departed Patriots, or even departed Loyalists, were promptly seized. Who, after all, could be sure whether the absentee was Patriot, Tory, or Traitor? Churches became hospitals, warehouses were cleared to house arms and war supplies, empty buildings in the harbor were put to use as prisons. Rents quadrupled, but rent control was effective by 1778. Despite inflation and shortages, New York City remained peaceful and prosperous through the seven years of war. This accomplishment was in no small measure due to the skill and patience of the British Commandant-General James

Robertson, and of Andrew Eliot, superintendent of the port and head of the police.

The Army was not always welcome. Isaac Heron, a watch-maker from Brooklyn, said that the rebels had plundered his property, but that the Hessians "complet'd his Ruin." As Wallace Brown has put it: "In short, the active Loyalist of New York City was a member of a substantial minority, was more probably wealthy than his fellow Loyalists in other parts of the State, was usually a long-standing immigrant from the British Isles and was more likely to be a merchant or shopkeeper than anything else."[8]

In fact, many merchants had been active Whigs and had been opposing British policies for at least a decade. But they were far more afraid of the turbulence of war and of the turbulence of mobs than they were of any British tyrant, if tyrant he was, who was at least 3,000 miles away. In her study, *New York Merchants on the Eve of the Revolution,* Virginia Harrington has described how merchants gradually lost control of the colonial protest and became what she called "eventual conservatives."[9]

Professor Robert East has also proved conclusively that at heart the New York City merchant class were for neutralism or Loyalism and that, had there been an active persecution of them, they would have been "decimated."[10] Thus Isaac Low, who was at the head of many committees of merchants and had until 1775 the confidence of both sides, drew a line at the idea of independence, and became both Loyalist and, later, claimant. Of the 104 members of the New York Chamber of Commerce living in 1775, 57 became Loyalists, 21 were neutral, and 26 became Whigs. Indeed, so many merchants were Loyalists that their exile in 1783 was impossible.

In the end many of them were quietly reabsorbed in the postwar city. But then, very few indeed, in New York City or outside it, were for independence before 1776. As late as October 1775, John Adams thought independence "a Hobgoblin of so frightening mien that it would throw a delicate person into Fits to look it in the Face." And after the Declaration of

Independence, no less than 704 New York City Loyalists known as the "Signers" petitioned General Howe in October 1776 asking for a restoration of civil law and attesting their loyalty to the Crown. Their petition was dubbed the Declaration of Dependence.

To these sources of Loyalism (recent immigration, Anglicanism in the church, and all the official ties with Britain that were the consequence of trade and government), there came a reinforcement from the refugees who poured into the city in 1778, after the evacuation of Philadelphia. More arrived in 1782–83, after the abandonment of Charleston and Savannah, and the population of the city grew quickly. It has been estimated that when Howe took possession in 1776 only 5,000 of its regular inhabitants remained. By February 1777, its civilian population had reached 11,000; by 1781, 25,000; and by the time of the final eviction in 1783, it was 33,000, in addition to the 10,000 British troops with their 25,000 dependents who were stationed there.

When in June 1775 the royal Governor and George Washington entered New York on the same day, both received escorts and both were cheered in the streets, probably by the same crowd. New York City, then, as always, was a law unto itself. But it was at least less pretentious than Boston. The Bostonians, said Samuel Seabury, thought that "God had made Boston for himself, and all the rest of the world for Boston."

The reaction of New York City to the coming of the Revolution at least confirms that Loyalism was not a class phenomenon. Although most members of the Establishment were Loyalists, nevertheless it is not possible to sustain any analysis of Loyalism exclusively by social class and by occupation. The Tories included many who were weavers and cobblers, laborers and shopkeepers. Those arrested in New York in June 1776 on suspicion of plotting to kill George Washington included the Mayor of New York, farmers, tavern-keepers, a shoemaker, two doctors, two tanners, a silversmith, a saddler, laborers, two gunsmiths, a miller, a tallow-chandler, a former schoolmaster, a pensioner with one arm, and an unfortunate man described only as "a damned rascal."

What, then, were the strands in the Loyalism of New York State? A number can clearly be indentified. First, New York was a key point in the strategic line of communication with Canada: via Manhattan Island, the Hudson Valley, the Mohawk Valley, and Lake Champlain. As a result, it witnessed the Saratoga campaign in 1777, a decisive turning point in the war. On the frontier, Sir William Johnson, Col. John Butler, and the Indians were active all through the war years down to the Loyalist defeat at Johnstown in October 1781. This aspect of the Revolution has constantly either been minimized, or seen as particularly dastardly. In fact, however, from 1763 onward successive British Governments had consistently sought to protect the Iroquois in their possession of their hunting grounds west of the Appalachians, and to halt the westward drift of land speculators and settlers. First, by the Proclamation of 1763, then by the Treaty of Fort Stanwix in 1768, the Government and notably its Superintendent for Indian Affairs had acted imaginatively and skillfully.

The Iroquois also appreciated the muskets, equipment, and largesse Sir William Johnson dispensed at Johnson Hall in the Mohawk Valley. Sir William died in 1774 during a conference at Johnson Hall, at which he had sought to prevent the Iroquois going to the aid of the Shawnee, whose hunting lands Governor Dunmore of Virginia was threatening to invade. The Patriots sought to win over the Iroquois to their side but they stayed firmly Loyalist. When in late July 1777 Barry St. Leger moved through the valley, he was accompanied by 300 Mohawks led by Joseph Brant and 200 Senecas led by Butler. They were, however, hesitant and quarrelsome as well as savage allies. The Wyoming Valley and Cherry Valley massacres were but part of the price paid for their support; Loyalist farms and farmers as well as Patriot were ravaged and destroyed. When the war was over Brant led 1,800 Mohawks to a new home in Ontario.

Second, New York had a very large component of royal

officials, "friends of the Government," "men of business," "men of connection." The Claims Commission figures reveal that an army of royal officials resided in New York. Among them were Governor Tryon himself; Chief Justice William Smith (accepting that for this purpose he can be described as a Tory and not as an ex-Whig); judges of the Supreme Court like Thomas Jones and George Duncan Ludlow; John Tabor Kempe, the Attorney General; Robert Bayard, Judge of Admiralty; Beverley Robinson, still described as "of Virginia" though, of course, of New York State, and marrying into the Philipse clan; James DeLancey, and so on.

To them, and those who thought like them, Locke had a different meaning than he did to Sam Adams and Jefferson. They saw the Empire as a single state, geographically but not politically divided, with its government established by the Constitution; to deny the established authority of any part of the government was to destroy the whole. Daniel Leonard clearly saw, as he wrote in 1774, that to deny the authority of Parliament was to destroy the framework of the Constitution and with it the "priceless claim" to all the rights guaranteed by that Constitution. On the same reasoning, Samuel Seabury labeled the Whig contention that the colonists owed allegiance not to Parliament but to the King a self-contradictory heresy:

> It is a distinction made by the American republicans to serve their own rebellious purpose, a gilding with which they have enclosed the pill of sedition. . . . The king of Great Britain was placed on the throne by virtue of an act of parliament . . . And if we disclaim that authority of parliament which made him our king, we, in fact reject him from being our king,—for we disclaim that authority by which he is king at all.

But if there was a strong sense of loyalty among officials, there was an even more compelling sense of loyalty among landowners. The large landed proprietors of New York were "at heart and by habit true aristos and denunciators of the

democratic movement," to quote A. C. Flick; "they were loyal
to the Crown because of received and anticipated favours."[11]
Not all wealthy landowners were Loyalist; the Van Cortlandts
were presumably as conscientious and sincere in their judgment as was Frederick Philipse III in his. Nevertheless, loyalty
to the Crown was a basic interest of and indeed an obligation on
the majority of the large landowners.

One of the most prominent of the Hudson Valley grandees
was Frederick Philipse himself. His estate extended over
90,000 acres and for 24 miles up the Hudson. He was a militia
colonel and, for twenty-five years, a member of the New York
Assembly. In the best feudal tradition, he was a good landlord,
conscientious, paternalistic, and sincere. "The rents were very
regularly paid every year," he told the Claims Commissioners.
"They were rather acknowledgements than rents. He should
[that is, could] have doubled his rents with great ease."

In contrast to Cortlandt's Manor, Philipsburg was in the sole
possession of the head of the Philipse family; when in 1784 he
was asked whether he had possessed "absolute" title to
Philipsburg Manor before the Revolution, he responded, according to the third-person record of the testimony, that "he
does not well know how to give a regular answer. In some sense
it might be said not . . . and yet he must certainly look on him
(self) as the proprietor. He could not turn off a tenant because
he did not like his face but he had at the same time the power of
raising their rent, which was tantamount to it." In fact he had
more than 270 tenant farmers, each of whom had on the
average some 200 acres. When he inherited his Manor in 1751
he persuaded his tenants to accept a modest increase in rents in
return for a promise not to raise them again in his lifetime.

At a time, especially in Dutchess County, when tenant riots
were familiar occurrences, in part because of the incursions
into New York of Yankee Squatters, his skill seemed com-
mendable and successful. But it all availed him little. He was
imprisoned, with great distress, in Connecticut in 1776;
he spent the war in New York City; and in 1783 he took refuge
in Britain. His Yonkers mansion was a British headquarters

throughout the war and in 1783 the entire estate was confiscated and sold. Tenants had been given a pre-emptive right to purchase the land they occupied, if they proved, on the evidence of twelve reliable witnesses, that they had taken an "active and decided part" in the Revolution. In 1785 this proof was abandoned, for those who could pay for their estates in cash, or by taking out a mortgage. Philipsburg is in other words a model of the Revolutionary transition from feudalism to democracy. As Beatrice Reubens says, "The immediate effect of the sale by the state, was to displace one wealthy and powerful landlord who had ruled over 50,000 acres and more than 270 tenants, and install 287 independent owners with an average holding of 174 acres. Moreover, at least 194 of the new owners, or well over two-thirds of the total, bought farms they had previously worked as tenants or inherited from tenants."[12]

Elsewhere the story was more violent and the roles reversed. The Livingston clan owned 160,000 acres in Albany County, and their Manor had been the scene in 1766 of a bitter clash between the Lord of the Manor and some 200 tenants. As Staughton Lynd writes, "Livingston Manor became a microcosm of the struggle over who should rule at home. The landlords were the traditional leaders of the anti-British party in the state; the tenants were New York's most obdurate malcontents. Where Landlords were Tories, as in neighboring Dutchess County, tenant uprisings could be harnessed to the Revolution, . . . but on Livingston Manor, where the landlords were prominent Whigs, the tenants became vigorous Tories."[13]

Prominent among them also was of course Sir John Johnson of the Mohawk Valley. And here again one notices the feudalism that still prevailed. When Sir John left for Canada in May 1776, he took 175 of his followers with him; and of these, no less than 149 put in claims for losses. Of this number, twenty were American-born, but three were English, seven were Irish, twenty-three were German, and no less than ninety-two were Scots. Indeed, of these ninety-two, seventy-two had arrived as recently as 1773. If there is some evidence that Loyalism was strongest where feudalism was strong, it is equally in evidence among those English-speaking groups who came late to American shores. The Loyalists, in other words, were often actual or potential aliens before they realized that they would have to make up their minds.

A third strand in Loyalism is exemplified in New York by Peter Van Schaack, William Smith, and in some measure by James Rivington, the editor of the outspokenly pro-British *New York Gazetteer*. They can be described as intellectuals, or perhaps as "conscience Whigs." They believed in Locke and the social contract, but not in the use of force. A clear line must be drawn, they held, between monarchy and tyranny. To many the clash between colony and Mother Country was an acute philosophical as well as a personal dilemma. Van Schaack retired to his country home at Kinderhook in January 1776 to read Locke's *Two Treatises on Government*, and to attempt to find his own acceptable middle ground.

To obviate the ill effects of either extreme, some middle way should be found out, by which the benefits to the empire should be secured arising from the doctrine of a supreme power, while the abuses of that power to the prejudice of the colonists should be guarded against; and this, I hope, will be the happy effect of the present struggle. . . . I cannot see any principle of regard for my country which will authorize me in taking up arms, as absolute *dependence* and *independence* are two extremes which I would avoid; for, should we succeed in the latter, we shall still be in a sea of uncertainty, and have to fight among ourselves for that constitution we aim at. . . . It is a question of morality and religion in which a man cannot conscientiously take an active part without being convinced in his own mind of the justice of the cause; . . . whatever disagreeable consequences may follow from dissenting from the general voice, yet I cannot but remember that I am to render an account of my conduct before a more awful tribunal, where no man can be justified who stands accused by his own conscience of taking part in measures which, through the distress and bloodshed of his fellow-creatures, may precipitate his country into ruin.[14]

Many sympathetic to American claims also wanted to stop short of total independence and certainly short of violence. The line between them was equally difficult to draw: Van Schaack and William Smith became Loyalists, John Jay and Gouverneur Morris stayed Patriot. Yet all of them came from similar backgrounds; and Morris, like many a Tory, recognized that "freedom and religion are only watchwords." Jemmy Rivington may as an editor have found the dividing line especially difficult to draw. He may well have been a double agent. But, unlike many others, in the end he returned to New York, and survived.

Of this category William Smith is the most interesting. The able and ambitious heir in 1767 to his father's position on the Governor's Council, historian and editor, lawyer and land speculator in the New Hampshire Grants, he had at first favored an American Parliament, as had Galloway. He had, like Franklin, a rosy vision of America's future.

> One cannot take the state, nature, climates, and prodigious extent of the American continent into contemplation without high prospects in favor of the power to which it belongs. It is sufficient to be the granary of all of the rest of the British dominions. Fed by our plough Britain might attend more to the cultivation of sheep, . . . the collection of raw materials from us and by us, . . . convert her own nation, as it were, into one great town of manufacturers, undersell every other nation in Europe and exalt and maintain her supremacy until heaven blots out the empires of the world.[15]

But he strove constantly to reconcile the irreconcilable. He called himself "a Whig of the old stamp . . . one of King Williams's Whigs, for liberty and the Constitution." It was a difficult position to sustain. His country home at Haverstraw was plundered. He obtained permission to go to New York

City in June 1778 to confer with the Carlisle Commission, and he moved deftly toward Loyalism. His biographer, L. F. S. Upton, has brilliantly traced the story of that skillful and tortured progression. He never ceased being a dissenter, says Upton. "He was incapable of steering a straightforward course, and surrounded every act with so many reservations and calculations that he rendered himself impotent in practical politics."[16] But his devious and worthy path, like that of Van Schaack, reveals how difficult it was for moderate and rational men not only to reconcile the two positions but to find a legitimate source of authority in a newly emerging society.

But it is false to Loyalism to see it only as a variant of Whiggism. The Loyalist was in essence a man or woman with a strong, if sometimes a quiet, devotion to the Mother Country and to the Establishment. Nor was it a matter merely of calculation, property and self-interest, as it was, in part, with William Smith. For many it was rooted not only in notions of deference in politics but of obedience to authority in religion. For the majority of Loyalists were first and last Anglicans. Nine Anglican clerics submitted claims, five American, three British, and one German. One of these, Charles Inglis of New York City, took his whole congregation of 2,000 with him to Nova Scotia when he went into exile.

It is unwise to minimize the power of the ideas of authority and obedience that lay behind Loyalism and Conservatism. "I believe," "I obey," these were part of the Loyalist code. Certainly in the eighteenth century, and perhaps until very recently, a strong religious sanction lay behind the idea of being loyal to the Monarch, because the Monarch in turn was loyal to and was first servant of God. These nine Anglican clerics were key figures in the Loyalist story. As in the views of Duché and Boucher, they showed not only respect for the Church but distrust of the Yankee, and of the Congregationalist, and awareness that a century earlier those who had shouted "No Bishop" had usually added "No King." In his memorial to the Claims Commissioners, Charles Inglis gave the reasons for his loyalty as attachment to the king, attachment to the British

constitution, "the best political fabric that ever existed," and a
desire to defend the church of England,

> which naturally results from a full conviction that her doc-
> trines and plan of Government are conformable to Holy
> Scripture and that her Spirit are more libral [sic] and mild
> than that of any other Christian Church whatever. [Before
> the Revolution] the Americans were . . . in possession of as
> large a portion of freedom as could well consist with a state of
> Civil Society—that if they were not happy the want of
> liberty was not cause, they could not change but for the
> worse—and that a separation of the colonies from the parent
> State must be highly injurious perhaps ruinous to both
> Countries.

To some of these men, like Myles Cooper, president of
King's College from 1763 to 1773, the struggle called for an
American Bishopric and an Anglican University, as part of an
attempt to restore that harmony, balance, and unity that were
the basis of social order. In their newspaper essays, *A Whip for
the American Whig*, Cooper and Inglis tapped a Burkeian
notion of order. Because the "advantages of honesty and
obedience to government" do not automatically "restrain the
sallies of ambition or the unresisted desire of unlimited freedom," only the prospect of ultimate divine judgement, "re-
wards" for "virtue and punishment of vice," can ensure the
operation of "that *order* and *harmony* so requisite to the just
motion in the springs of every political system." These men
sensed the "frensy" that was at work below the Patriot surface.
In his *Patriot of North America* he wrote:

> Behold a vain, deluded Race,
> Thy venerable Name, disgrace;
> As Casuists false, as Savage rude,
> With Glosses weak, with Comments crude,
> Pervert thy fair, instructive Page,
> To Sanctify licentious Rage.

"Party heat, the fever of Liberty," wrote Samuel Seabury, "may vitiate the mind as much as jaundice does the eyes." A parody published in New York in 1775, *The Triumph of the Whigs*, put it even more bluntly. "Rouse, therefore, my friends! Support the Congress and assert your *native* rights of doing as you please. Your only danger will arise from . . . failing. . . . In that case you will indeed be *rebels* and may chance to be hanged. But if you *succeed*, it will only be a *revolution*, and you will be justified before God and man. Nothing . . . was wanting to make Lucifer's rebellion in Heaven *a glorious revolution* but success." Thomas Bradbury Chandler of New Jersey asked "whether . . . the supreme governor of the world . . . has given any dispensation to the body of the people, under any government, to refuse *honor* or *custom* or *tribute* to whom they are due; to contract habits of thinking and *speaking evil of dignities*, and to weaken the natural principle of respect for those in authority"? Oliver Parker of New Hampshire went to jail for composing:

a recipe to make a Whig: Take of conspiracy and the root of pride three handfuls, two of ambition and vain glory. Pound them in the mortar of faction and discord. Boil it in 3 quarts of dissembling tears and a little New England rum over the fire of sedition until you find the scum of falsehood to rise to the top. Then strain it through the cloth of rebellion, put it into the bottle of envy, stop it with the cork of malice. . . .

and so on until the mixture had been made into pills, swallowed at bedtime, and the "next day. . .you will be thinking how to cozzen, cheat, lie, and get drunk, abuse the minister of the gospel, cut the throats of all honest men, and plunder the nation."

Anglicanism was thus the bedrock of Loyalism. Discipline, order and hierarchy in the Church supported discipline, order, and hierachy in the State. As Edward Bass put it, "As . . . members of society, we are all obliged in point of honor, interest, and conscience to maintain its security, promote its welfare, and guard it against any factious or seditious conspiracies."

The bands of society would be dissolved, the harmony of the world confounded, and the order of nature subverted, Chandler warned, if reverence, respect, and obedience might be refused to those whom the constitution had vested with the highest authority. *The ill-consequences of open disrespect to government are so great that no misconduct by the administration can justify or excuse it.*"

One further element figured in New York Loyalism: Upstate New York was Indian country. As we have seen, Brant and his Mohawks were loyal to Britain largely out of loyalty to the Johnson clan, who had for two generations dominated the Mohawk Valley. The civil war fought by the Indians was bitter and ugly; and as a result, Colonel Butler and his Rangers became folk villains. The War of Independence was not only a civil war but a guerrilla war. Ironically it made heroes of some of them, like Marion and Sumter, and particular villains of others, like Butler; yet they were all doing the same thing, only on different sides. This was, however, a revolution, and it was fought by other rules than those of European warfare.

It was a civil war too in other respects. Not only was it a struggle between Home Country and an overseas colony. It was, especially in New York, one of continuing rivalries between major families, notably in the form of Royalists and Loyalists (the DeLanceys) versus Patriots (the Livingstons). It was, as Carl Becker put it, a struggle over who should rule at home, a struggle for power. In all politics power is the name of the game. This explains why both sides had been, up to 1775, Whig. The statistician has now intruded and made it possible for us to see that it was a struggle between elites, a struggle within a ruling class.

It was not a revolution of levelers, but rather of an upper class, who believed that all men should be equal to compete for the inequality of office and honor. The Patriots were usually a little younger than those who became Loyalists, and were

more likely to have been educated in America than in England.
The Loyalists on the other hand came mainly from families
with colonial-imperial connections. Sixty percent of executive
Loyalists, claims James Kirby Martin,[17] came from elite
backgrounds in contrast to 31 percent of the Revolutionary
executives. And the departure of these native-born Loyalists,
along with the British appointees, opened up, at least for that
generation, coveted political posts. The Revolutionary governments elected their governors and called for the direct
election of senators. A new world came into being.

> If ponies rode men, and if grass ate the cows,
> And cats should be chased into holes by the mouse,
> If summer were spring and the other way around,
> Then all the world would be upside down.

That was the sentiment and those were the words ostensibly to
which the British marched out to surrender at Yorktown. It was
indeed a world turned upside down. It was the first real civil
war, one of the first of urban and rural guerrilla wars, and the
first crack in the edifice, up to then the noble edifice, and now
perhaps only a noble and nostalgic dream, of the British Empire.

What then of New York Loyalists in the Revolution? They
were significant, for there were in the state as a whole more of
them than anywhere else, and especially so in New York City.
They were more varied than Loyalists elsewhere: officials and
lawyers and men of connection, but ordinary folk too; wealthy
patrons like the Philipses and the DeLanceys, but also recently
arrived tenant farmers on the Hudson or the Mohawk; Anglicans, Presbyterians, and Dutch Reformed; a number of slaves
and free blacks; Indians, Indian traders, and speculators in
Indian lands, a cross-section indeed of American life. William
H. Nelson has demonstrated, in *The American Tory*,[18] that the
Tory rank-and-file "represented conscious minorities, people
who felt weak and threatened . . . [who] were in one way or

another more afraid of America than they were of Britain [and] had interests they felt needed protection from an American majority."

The New York Loyalists thus pose more sharply than elsewhere the key question: Why were they militarily of so little account, and why was so little use made of them? Plainly the British Government paid small attention to them, and indeed to "the people" as such. For the British Government saw the war in terms of trained regulars versus ill-organized militia, and had no doubt which would win. We know that the future was not on their side, and we in the twentieth century have more reason for knowing that from now on all wars are likely to take on a similar guerrilla, militia, and partisan form. Of this, New York in the Neutral Ground, and bloodily in the Mohawk Valley, provided all too much evidence.

For the rest, the Loyalist story is a story of diaspora and defeat. It is full of the anguish and heartache of all exile, of new homes in bleak surroundings, of United Empire Loyalists, of nostalgia and sentiment which surrounds so much Canadian history, and so much Scottish legendry. But American history proves to be a different history, Whig not Tory; popular, and at times populist, not aristocratic; Jacksonian, not Jeffersonian or Hutchinsonian; open not closed.

The Americans lost their Establishment and have never quite found a replacement for it. Of course, the Revolution and the separation from Britain need not have happened, for all events can be controlled, directed, and steered, and by men. The Loyalists suffered because of a failure of British statesmanship, skill, and understanding, and because of a misreading of the nature of war in the eighteenth century. If a few things had been done differently, if the Home Government had listened to Ben Franklin, if it had given George Washington a regular commission twenty years earlier, if General Howe had moved with vigor in 1776, if . . . But it did not do so. And it paid a heavy price.

Appendix
A Loyalist Claim: The Philipse Estate

M ANY AMERICAN LOYALISTS whose properties were confiscated or forfeited sought to obtain compensation from the British Government for the losses they had incurred. After a great deal of political maneuvering, the Loyalists were successful in moving the Crown to establish a Royal Commission of Enquiry to hear their claims. Voluminous records were subsequently compiled by the Commission between 1784 and 1786, containing general information on the way of life in the former North American colonies, testimony from the unfortunate Loyalists, massive supportive documentation, and a multiplicity of corroborating statements from witnesses familiar with the people and properties involved.

In the last decade of the nineteenth century, The New York Public Library undertook the major task of transcribing many of these records and making them available to scholars. This was followed by the publication in 1915 of Hugh E. Egerton's edited selections from the *Notes* of Daniel Parker Coke, one of the Royal Commissioners who sat on the Commission of Enquiry on the Losses and Services of American Loyalists.

Most recently, the original records concerned with the Loyalist claims, which had been classified as Audit Office Series 12 and 13 in H. M. Public Record Office, London, have been made available on microfilm. The labyrinthian path of a Loyalist claim from its inception to culmination can be followed through the magic of microfilm copies of such original documents.

In the case of Frederick Philipse III, and his son, Frederick Philipse IV, another dimension is added to the historical record with the availability of personal family copies of many of the documents submitted to the Commissioners. It is possible to check family copies against the filed documents in the Public Record Office and with The New York Public Library's transcripts as well as those in Egerton's edition of Coke's *Notes*. Immediately apparent even to the most casual reader is the variation in the spelling of names and places from one version to another. Wherever possible, the spellings appearing in the documents presented here follow the spellings found in the family copies, preserving the inconsistencies in the original documents.

The complete set of documents appears for the first time in this volume.

While most of the Philipse family personal and business correspondence records vanished either during or shortly after the American Revolution, the documentation supporting the Philipses' claims of losses remained intact within the family's possession until purchased by Sleepy Hollow Restorations. The historical richness of these documents provides a small clue to what family papers must have existed at an earlier time. Consolation lies in what yet remains in scattered repositories.

The documents included herein provide an account of one family's effort at obtaining monetary redress for their losses. It also portrays a way of life which already was on the edge of extinction at the time of the American Revolution.

Jacob Judd

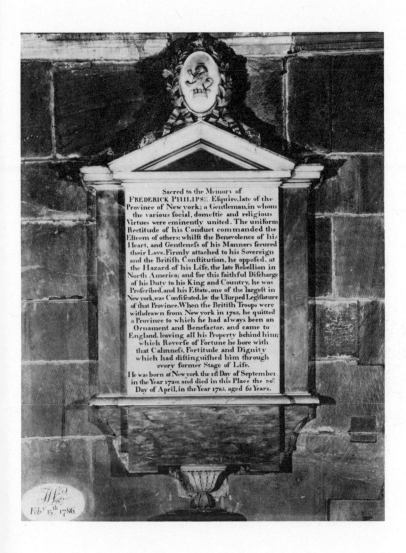

Inscription on the crypt of Frederick Philipse III,
Chester, England.

Members of Philipse Family Mentioned in Claims

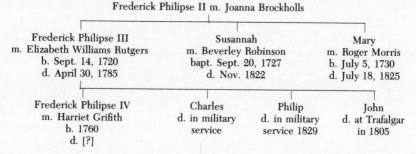

Frederick Philipse II m. Joanna Brockholls

Frederick Philipse III m. Elizabeth Williams Rutgers b. Sept. 14, 1720 d. April 30, 1785	Susannah m. Beverley Robinson bapt. Sept. 20, 1727 d. Nov. 1822		Mary m. Roger Morris b. July 5, 1730 d. July 18, 1825
Frederick Philipse IV m. Harriet Grifith b. 1760 d. [?]	Charles d. in military service	Philip d. in military service 1829	John d. at Trafalgar in 1805

Beverley Robinson, son-in-law to Frederick Philipse, was an active Loyalist participant in the military phase of the American Revolution. He raised a company of Loyalists and had served as their commander prior to being placed in secret service activities. His own Memorial to the Commission of Enquiry into the Losses and Services of the American Loyalists can be found in Volume 43 of the New York Public Library's *Transcript of the Manuscript Books and Papers of the Commission of Enquiry. . . . Examinations in London: Memorials, Schedules of Losses and Evidences: New York Claimants in six books (Book iii).*

His statement of real estate and slave values in the New York counties of the Hudson River Valley is of interest for the background information he provided.

New York currency was discounted in relation to British pounds sterling in varying degrees, depending upon economic and political circumstances. In the Philipse claims, the Commissioners discounted New York currency at the rate of £1.72 being equivalent to £1 sterling.

Sept. 12, 1783.

INFORMATION COMMUNICATED
to the COMMISSIONERS
by COLONEL ROBINSON.*

Value of
Land

A good piece of Land of 100 ª. of a cleared Land in Dutchess
county New York wo.ᵈ usually let for £30. currency- a Farm of
this kind would sell for 7 or 8.ˡ p acre currency- Its difficult to
settle any general value upon Land, it depends so much upon
Situation, Lands lying within 5 or 6 Miles of a Landing place
on a River was very valuable- Unsettled Lands of little value-
Believes there have been Lands sold before any Cultivation
upon them; but they have sold very low- Is of opinion the
Americans would hardly permit any Examination into the
State of Loyalists property in that country. Is convinced they
would not permit any thing to be done, in it at present,

Registers
in New
York

whatever they might in future.- Lands sold in New York
were registered in the Secretaries Office, which was for the
whole province, or in the Office of the Clerk of the particular
County- This was not compelled by Law but was regularly
done by the parties for their own Security- Believes Gen.ˡ
Tryon has most of the public papers- not one in 50 con-
veyances made in the middle provinces but was regularly

Negroes.

recorded- Few Negroes in New York in comparison of the
Southern Colonies- but few in a family- Paid about 4 Guineas
a year for Poors Rates of the precinct he lived in with a fifth

Value of
Lands.

part of the rate of the whole precinct. Many purchases before
the Troubles took place- Many people would sell old settled
Lands, for where they would sell high, in order to purchase
New Lands where they would get a much larger quantity and
a much lower Rate, no mode of ascertaining the value of
particular Estates which have been lost, but by the opinion
and valuation of other persons who knew the property- No
general rule of ascertaining the value of property- Thinks the
best mode will be by examinᵍ Witnesses upon Oath-There is
no Evidence upon Record of the value of Estates, only as to
the Title- Even the price of late purchases would be no
accurate Rule of estimatᵍ the value- The purchases being of

* Transcript of the Manuscript Books and Papers of the Commission of
Enquiry into the Losses and Services of the American Loyalists held
under Acts of Parliament of 23, 25, 26, 28 and 29 of George III. Preserved
amongst the Audit Office Records in the Public Record Office of England
1783–1790: Information and Intelligence conveyed to the Commissioners to prevent Imposition and Fraud 1782 to 1785. Volume I (New York
Public Library, 1898).

Confisca-
tions.

Value of
Negroes.

small convenient Tracts in general which sold higher than the real value- Most of the confiscated Estates were sold by Certificates granted to the Soldiery for their pays who were glad to sell their Certificates at a great depreciation of ten £5 for £100- This made them appear to sell greatly above what they really did- Believes where these confiscated Estates were personal Inventor.ˢ were taken but no appraisement made of real Estates- A good Negro before the War began was worth £50 Sterling- could not form any accurate guess as to the average value of Negroes, but thinks they might be about £40- a Head. No Tax or Assessm.ᵗ in the province of New York- M.ʳ Ludlow a Man of exceeding good Character & from his Situation very conversant in the value of Lands, was Judge of the supreme Court, and has very little Landed property of his own- M.ʳ Van Schaack a Barrister likewise able to give Information as to the value of Lands in New York- Col. Robinson will willingly give his Opinion as to the value of Lands in the province when he can do it accurately- Believes the Loyalists in general are pleased with the Attention paid to them by Government.

Appendix [101]

AN EARLY STATEMENT OF LOSSES SUSTAINED BY
FREDERICK PHILIPSE AS A RESULT
OF HIS ALLEGIANCE TO THE CROWN.*

[January, 1784]
Memorial of Frederic Philips Esqr late of West Chester County, Province of New York, North America, requesting immediate relief & subsistence for himself & Family [now residing in London] from the Honorable Board of Commissioners appointed for Enquiry into the losses sustained by the Loyalists of North America.

Humbly Sheweth

That your Memorialist having been obliged to leave said country in consequence of several acts of attainder issued by the Assembly of said Province, against his Person & Property, for his & Familys known attachment to the Royal cause, thereby loosing all his large Estate & Personal Fortune, as will be more particularly shewn in the Papers he is now preparing for said Honorable Boards consideration & Report; Your Petitioner therefore requests that he may receive such present subsistence as the Honorable Board may think adequate for the maintenance of himself & very large family, 'till the compensation in consequence of the Honorable Board's report takes place.

The Honorable Boards compliance with this memorial shall be gratefully acknowledged by their most obedient
and
Faithfull
Humble Servant
Fred Philips

* Audit Office Series 13 Volume 116, Public Record Office, London.

FREDERICK PHILIPSE'S CLAIMS FOR LOSSES SUPPORTED BY
FIVE INFLUENTIAL SIGNATORIES
TO A LETTER OF CHARACTER REFERENCE.*

January 29th 1784

We whose names are hereunto subscribed certify that Frederic Philips Esqr late of New York, was according to our knowledge, Information and Belief, possessed of considerable property of the first Magnitude in the Province of New York, of which he has been deprived in consequence of his Loyalty & a Steady Attachment to Great Britain, and we now understand Mr. Philips is come to England with His Lady & a very numerous Family, who have the misfortune to see him equally ruined in his Health & Circumstances, we Therefore believe Mr. Philips is peculiarly deserving of Immediate support & subsequent compensation,

Geo. Johnstone
[Earl of] Carlisle
James Robertson
Wm. Eden
Wm. Tryon.

* Audit Office Series 13 Volume 116, Public Record Office, London.

Appendix

To The Commissioners Appointed by Act of Parliament

For Inquiring Into The Losses and Services of

the American Loyalists*

The memorial of Frederick Philips, Esquire, respectfully showeth—

That your memorialist was one of the members of the legal assembly of the Province of New York from the year 1750 to 1775, in which he possessed during that time a considerable share of influence and uniformly opposed every measure there proposed, which he thought inconsistent with the rights of the Crown and Parliament, as may appear by the minutes more at lodge.

That from the time he perceived the late Tumults in America tended to weaken and destroy His Majesty's authority over it, actuated by the firmest principles of loyalty in attachment to the British Government he exerted his influence to prevent it, and particularly in the Spring 1776 he conveined a large number of the freeholders and inhabitants of the Town of West Chester and prevailed on them to enter into an Association to preserve the Peace and to support the legal government, but that his laudable intentions were frustrated by the superior force of several parties which were after formed in the County and others which came from Connecticut and at length the person of your memorialist was seized on by a party of American volunteers from New York, and carried from his family a prisoner into Connecticut, where he was confined for the space of six months. That being released from his confinement by a parole granted by Governor Trumbull, he made his escape with his family consisting at that time of a wife and nine children and sought for refuge within the British lines at New York.

That after his arrival within the British lines five of his sons entered into His Majesty's service for the purpose of assisting in reducing of the rebellion, and that for two of them, who have been since unfortunately lost in the said service, your memorialist purchased Commissions with money which he was obliged to borrow and for which with the interest he yet stands indebted to the persons who lent it.

That in consequence of the loyal part thus taken by your Memorialist and his Family the usurped legislature of New York passed a law for attainting his person and confiscating all his estate, both real and personal whereby he was totally deprived of a very valuable Estate of which he was seized of part as Tenant for Life, and part in Fee, specified in the Schedule hereunto annexed.

Your Memorialist therefore prays that you would take his case into your consideration and make such report thereon as shall enable him to obtain such Compensation for his Services and those Losses which he has sustained in consequence of his attachment to the British Government.

Fred Philips

* Philipse Family Papers in the Collections of Sleepy Hollow Restorations.

A SCHEDULE AND VALUATION OF THE ESTATE

OF FREDERICK PHILIPS ESQUIRE,

CONFISCATED BY THE ESTATE OF NEW YORK

LIFE ESTATE	NEW YORK CURRENCY	STERLING MONEY
1. Rent of the Real estate, houses thereon, and Manor, from 26th December, 1776 to 25th December, 1784, both inclusive. See the will, Rent Roll and Map.	21,960: 7:4	12,701: —:—
2. Rent of the mansion house, demesne, and part of the Mills where Mr. Philips formerly resided, from 26th December, 1776, to 26th December, 1784, both inclusive, at £600 per annum. See Will and Valuation.		4,800: —:—
3. Rent of 100 Acres of salt meadow situate in Orange County from 26th December, 1776 to 25th December, 1784 both inclusive at £100 per annum. See Will and Valuation.	800: —:—	450: —:—
4. Rent of Kingsbridge Island a house from 26th December, 1776 to 25th December 1784, both inclusive at £100 per annum. See Will and Valuation.	800: —:—	450: —:—
5. Value of a lot of land situate in New Street corner of Stone Street New York. See Will and Valuation.	1150: —:—	646:17:6
6. Value of a lot of land situate in New Street New York. See Will and Valuation.	75: —:—	42: 3:9
7. Loss of personal property to Mr. Philips. See particular (letter A) annexed.	1698:10:—	955: 8:—
8. Value of Mr. Philips's life estate in 1, 2, 3, 4.		11,223:19:1¾
9. Amount of Bonds and Notes with interest due thereon to the 25th December 1784. See particular (letter B) annexed.	15,890:13:7½	8,938:10:—

£42,374:10:11½

The Total Amount of Loss in
Sterling Money

£40,216:18:4¾

Appendix

Appendix   [105]

Rent Roll of Colonel Frederick Philips's Estate
In The Province of New York
Of Which He Was Possessed as Tenant For Life.

	New York Currency
Albert Artse, Jr.	6: 4:6
Lewis Angevine	6: 4:–
David Akerman	6: 4:–
William Artse	6: 4:–
John Artse	3: 4:–
Joseph Applebee	10:14:–
Caleb Archer	6:12:–
Richard Archer	2:10:–
Alexander Allaire	7: 4:6
Elbert Artse	4:14:6
Hendrick Brown	4:10:–
Elisha Barton	5: –:–
Peter Bonnett	9: –:–
Thomas Barker	4: –:–
Joshua Barnes	5:10:–
John Brown	2:10:–
Joshua Bishop	8:10:–
Thomas Buys	6: 4:6
John Basley	1:10:–
Nicholas Belle	30: –:–
Jacob Buys	3: 4:6
Abraham Brown	6: 4:6
Hendrick Banker	4:14:6
John Bullje	3: 4:6
John Basley	5: 4:6
Thomas Bishop	6: 4:6
John Buljie, Jr., Sing Sing	5: 4:6
Edward Bugbee	6: 4:6
Johannes Brown	6: 4:6
Johannes Bredt	3: 4:6
Arie Buys Peterson	15:10:9
Jacob Buckhout	6: 4:6
Arie Buys	6: 4:6
Matthew Brandt 12 Cider Casks	
Capt. John Brockhout	7: 4:6
Zephaniah Birdsel	7: 4:6
Jerimiah Baker	6: 4:6
Jonathan Baker	6: 4:6
Thomas Baker	2: 1:6
Benjamin Brown	6: 4:6
Gershom Bishop	6:10:
Thomas Browne	6:10:–

John Bates	5:10:–
Evert Brown	9: –:–
Michael Chatterton	6: 4:6
Thomas Champinois	6: 4:6
William Cornel	6: 4:6
David Conklin	6: 4:6
William Crawford	8:10
George Combes A Lot	1: 5:–
Joseph Conklin	2:10:–
James McChain	11:17:–
John Cock (for the house at Kingsbridge)	100: –:–
Augustus Van Cortlandt	5: –:–
Peter Davids	6: 4:6
William Deane	4:12:–
William David	5:14:6
Samuel Deane	9: 4:6
Widow of John Davenport	6: 4:6
Johannes Dutcher	7: 4:6
Issaac Deane	6: 4:6
Abraham Devous	3: 4:6
Daniel Devous	6:10:–
Fred Devous	6:10:–
John Dusenberg	7:12:–
David Davids	5:14:6
Jacobus Davids	3:14:6
Robert Dickensen	1: 7:6
Samuel Desborough	3:10:–
Samuel Deans carpenter	1: –:–
Harman Davids	1: 5:–
Stephen Ecker Stephanson	5: 4:6
Abraham A. Ecker	7: 4:6
Abraham Ecker, Sing Sing	5: 4:6
John Enters	6: 4:6
William Ecker	7: 4:6
Abraham Ecker	1: 5:–
Wolvert Ecker	2: –:–
Stephen Ecker	3: –:–
William Fisher	6: 4:6
William Fauchier	5: 4:6
John Fisher	8:16:–
Jeremiah Fisher	6: 4:6
William Field	5: 4:6
Benjamin Fowler	13:12:6
Matthew Farrington	4: 4:6
John Fauchier	6: 4:6
Peter Fauchier	7: –:–

Appendix

John Gibbs	7: 4:6
Marvil Garrison	5: 4:6
John Griffin	5: 4:6
Absalom Gedney	5:10:–
Isaac Greene	5:16:–
William Haight	4: 2:6
Israel Honeywell	7: –:–
John Hall	5:14:6
Jonathan Horton	5:14:6
Staats Hammond	2: 1:6
James Hill	15:19:–
John Hogencamp	8: –:–
Gilbert Hatfield	6: 4:6
William Hunt	8:14:6
Jonathan P. Horton	6: 4:6
Arnold Hunt	5:14:6
Gilbert Horton	6: 4:6
Peter Heck	3: 4:6
John Hammond	5:14:6
Samuel Huestede's Widow	4: 4:6
James Hammond	6: 4:6
Caleb Huested	6: 4:6
John Hunt	6: 4:6
Samuel Horton	6: 4:6
James Hunter's Widow	6: 4:6
Samuel Haight	6: 4:6
Ebijah Haight	6: 4:6
Isaac Hammond	6: 4:6
George Hadely	10: –:
Solomon Huested	6:10:–
Joshua Hunt	6:10:–
Elnathan Hunt	6:10:–
Joseph Hart	5:10:–
Thomas Hyatt	9: –:–
William Jefferies	3: 4:6
Cornelius Jones	4: 4:6
Arthur Jones	2:14:6
Benjamin Jenkins	15: 4:6
Jacob Cortwright	4:10:–
Michael Kortwright	2:10:–
Hendrick Kronkheyt	3: 4:6
Lewis Kniffin	5:14:6
Richard Kenniff	3: 4:6
Elisha Leggatt	6: 4:6
Joseph Legget	6: 4:6
Widow of Elisha Legget	6: 4:6

Abraham Ladue	3: 4:6
Underhill Lynch	3: 4:6
Isaac Lawrence	5:10:–
Isaac Lawrence, Jr.	6: 1:8
Adrian LaForge	7: –:–
Henry LaForge	7: –:–
Jacob Lent	5:10:–
Hendrick Lambert	3:10:–
Barent LeMatre	5:14:6
John Martine	15: 6:3
Annanias Matthews	3:10:–
Elisha Merrit	3: 4:6
Elijah Miller	2: 6:–
Daniel Mertlings a lot	1: 5:–
George Monson a lot	1: 5:–
Moses Millar	6: 4:6
Daniel Millar	2: –:–
Abraham Mertlings, Jr.	1: 5:–
Jonathan Odell	15:14:6
Thomas Oakley	2:10:–
Moses Oakley	4:5:–
Caleb Oakley	6: 4:6
William Van Orstrandt	3:14:6
Joseph Oakley	6:10:–
The Widow of John Odell	6:10:–
Joshua Odell	7: –:–
Michael Odell	7:12:–
John Odell, His Son	4:5:–
John Oakley	2: 2:6
John Oakley	5:14:6
Gabriel Purdy	3:14:6
James Purdy	2:12:6
Peter Post	7: –:–
David Pugsley	6:10:–
Samuel Purdy	5: 4:6
Samuel Purdy, Jr.	5:14:6
James Pearce	5:14:6
Jacob Post	6:10:–
Isaac Post	10:10:–
Widow of H. Post	6: –:–
Gilbert Pugsley	6:10:–
Joseph Paulding	6: 4:6
William Pugsley	200: –:–
Isaac Reade	3: 4:6
Jacob Rider	6: 4:6
Hode Requa	12: 4:6

Daniel Requa	6: 4:6
James Requa	10:14:–
Joshua Rich	3:10:–
Robert Reade	5:10:–
John Requa	3:15:6
Jacob Roomer	–:16:–
Thomas Rich	6:10:–
Isaac Sie	5: 4:6
John Smith	6:10:–
Caleb Smith	3:15:–
Conrade Sidore	–:16:–
John Storm, Jr.	15: –:–
Solomon Sherwood	5:14:6
Gersham Sherwood	3:14:6
Jasper Stymets	11: –:–
John Storm	6: 4:6
John Shute	5: 4:6
Widow Sypher	6: 4:6
Hendrick Storm	6: 4:6
Jacob Sie	6: 4:6
Abram Storm	12: 4:6
Abram N. Storm	6: 4:6
David Sie	6: 4:6
Nicholas Storm	6: 4:6
Jeremiah Stivers	4:14:6
Joshua Sherwood	4: 4:6
Thomas Sherwood	6:10:–
Stephen Sherwood	2: –:–
Jeremiah Sherwood	5:10:–
Job Sherwood	6: 4:6
John Smith	6: 4:6
Peter Sypher	3:10:–
Nathaniel T. Tompkins	6:10:–
Jacob Van Tessel Johnson	5: 4:6
John Townsend, Jr.	6:10:–
Nehemia Tompkins	5: –:–
Thomas Tompkins	6:15:6
Uriah Traverse	6: 4:6
David Van Texel	6: 4:6
Peter Van Texel	6: 4:6
Cornelius Van Texel	6: 4:6
John Tompkins	5:10:–
Benjamin Taylor	5:10:–
Jacob Van Texel	3: 4:6
Elijah Tompkins	7: 4:6
John Tompkins, Jr.	6: 4:6

Widow Tompkins	5: 4:6
Elnathan Taylor	6:10:–
Nathaniel Tompkins	6: 4:6
John Van Texel Johnson	5: 4:6
Gilbert Tompkins	5: 4:6
John Van Texel	6: 4:6
William Tompkins	2: –:–
Isreal Underhill	150: –:–
John Vincent	7:12:–
William Underhill	11:11:–
Nathaniel Underhill, Jr.	9: 1:9
Abraham Underhill	10:19:–
Jacob Underhill	5: 4:6
Benjamin Underhill	3: 4:6
Samuel Underhill	3: 4:6
Widow of John Underhill	6:10:–
John Underhill, Jr.	5: 4:6
Widow of A. Vallentine	6:10:–
Thomas Valentine	5:10:–
Mathias Valentine	5:10:–
Isaac Vermilljie	6:10:–
Jacob Vermilljie	6:10:–
Benjamin Vermilljie	6: 4:6
William Underhill	1:15:–
Daniel Winter	3: 4:6
Thomas Willy	12:9:–
Arie Van Wormer	3: 4:6
Martinus Van Wert	6: 4:6
Widow of William Van Wert	6: 4:6
Jacob Van Wert	6: 4:6
John Van Wert	7: 4:6
Gilbert Ward	12:9:–
Abram Williams	5:14:6
Richard Washbourn	5:10:–
John Warner	10:12:–
Widow of C. Warner	6:10:–
Thomas Ward	6: 4:6
Widow of Daniel Williams	2:12:–
Joseph Artse	4:15:–
Harman Williams	2: 4:6
Thomas Weeks a Lot	1: 5:–
Henry Van Wert	1:15:–
William Yorkse	16:12:–
Joseph Youngs	6: 4:6
John Yourks	6: 4:6
James Youngs	3:10:–

Thomas Hill	
a house on Dock Street, New York	100: –:–
Charles Hart Dock St., N.Y.	100: –:–
John McCord	6: 4:6
Abram Odell	11: –:–

Mr. Philips by Agreement
with his Tenants was intitled
upon every transfer to certain
fines which upon an Average
Amounted to £500 per annum   500: –:–

Total Currency   £2745: 0:11

Total Amount in Sterling Money   £1588:15:–

A copy of a List of Bonds and Notes

due to Frederick Philips Esquire as deposed before and
Certified by a Notary of New York with the Interest accrued
due thereon to the 25th day of December 1784 in New York
Currency and reduced to Sterling Money at the Sums Total or End.
Being the particular (Letter B) referred to by the Schedule
annexed to the Memorial.[1]

When payable	By whom executed	Principal	Principal received	When received	Interest received	Total Principal due on 25th Dec 1784	Total Interest due on 25th Dec 1784
1777 June 27	Josiah Hunt c[um] John Merritt	100	......	......	......	100	52 17 9
1777 June 10	John Buljie	100	......	......	......	100	52 15 11
1777 May 19	Daniel Billings c[um] John Merritt	125	......	......	......	125	67 4 ..
1777 May 17	Ch.s Vincent	100	......	......	......	100	53 4 11
1777 May 10	Sam.l Purdy Jun.r	40	......	......	......	40	21 7 8
1777 May 12	Joseph Cornell	100	......	......	......	100	53 6 10
1777 May 7th	Gilbert & Elnathan Taylor	155 5 ..	......	......	......	115 5 ..	62 19 9

1777 May 6	Lewis Heustis c[um] Ab.m Gedney	. . . . . .	100 . . .	53 9 4
1776 Ap.l 20	Benjamin Lewis	. . . . . .	200 . . .	121 11 ..
1776 May 3	John Fisher	. . . . . .	200 . . .	121 1 ..
1776 Ap.l 20	Henry & Samuel Purdy	7	100 . . .	53 15 6
1776 Ap.l 4th	Lewis M.c Donald Jun.r Esq.re	. . . . . .	251 6 8	154 13 ..
1776 Ap.l 20	Jonathan Purdy c[um] Isaac Oakley	. . . . . .	200 . . .	121 11 ..
1776 June 9th	Ruben Wright	. . . . . .	164 . . .	86 12 2
Carried forward		1895 11 8 / 7	1896 11 .. / 7	1076 6 2

[end of a ledger page]

1. From the Philipse Family Papers in the Collections of Sleepy Hollow Restorations. There are variations in the Christian names of those who executed bonds when this document is compared to another copy of the same list which appears in the transcripts of the American Loyalists Examinations prepared for the New York Public Library.

[new ledger page]

When payable	By whom executed	Principal	Principal received	When received	Interest received	Total Principal due on 25th Dec 1784	Total Interest due on 25th Dec 1784
	Brought forward	1895 11 8			7 ...	1895 11 8	1076 6 2
1776 May 1st	John Hogen Camp [?]	50 ...	......	....	.....	50 ...	38 5 7
1776 May 1st	John Stonn	100 ...	......	....	7 ...	100 ...	53 11 3
1765 Apl 3d	Jonathan Budd	300 ...	87 ...	1778 Aug 8	42 ...	213 ...	95 16 6
1775 May 7	William Yorkse	100 ...	......	....	14	100 ...	53 8 11
1774 May 1st	William Yourske	80 ...	......	....	11 4 ..	80 ...	37 4 10
1774 Apl 20	William Yourkse	100 ...	......	....	21 ...	100 ...	56 4 1
1776 May 1st	Elijah Hunter c[um] Jonathan Platt	160 ...	......	....	11 4 ..	160 ...	85 14 8
1775 May 1st	Peter Post	100 ...	......	....	14 ...	100 ...	53 6 ..
1775 Novr 10th	Peter Say Chrr Isenhart c[um] Josha Purdy	102 6 8	......	....	.....	102 6 8	65 6 ..
1775 Apl 5th	James McChain	100 ...	......	....	14 ...	100 ...	54 .. 9

1775 May 2d	James McChain	100 . . .	:	14 . .	100 . . .	53 10 8
1775 May 3d	Thomas Tompkins	100 . . .	:	:	100 . . .	67 10 3
1775 May 1st	John Bishop Junr	128 8 .	:	17 17 4	128 8 .	65 3 2
1775 Apl 13	Joel Warning c[um] Zephamiah Mills	50 . . .	:	:	50 . . .	33 18 10
1775 May 12	James c[um] Isaac Gidney	180 . . .	80 . . . . . 1776 June 13th	24 4 . .	100 . . .	59 14 9
1775 May 13	Ely Seely c[um] Jonathan Tyler	100 . . .	:	:	100 . . .	67 6 7
1774 May 4	Stephen & David Wering	50 . . .	:	3 10 . .	50 . . .	33 15 6
1774 May 11	Ephraim Raymond	100 . . .	:	14 . . .	100 . . .	60 7 2
1774 May 1st	Soloman Sherwood	50 . . .	:	:	50 . . .	37 5 6
1774 Apl 6	Gilbert Ward	76 7 6	:	12	76 7 6	44 14 10
	Carried forward	£4022 13 10	167	226 19 4	3855 13 10	2184 12 . .
					Error	8
						2192 15 6

[end of ledger page]

[new ledger page]

When payable	By whom executed	Principal	Principal received	When received	Interest received	Total Principal due on 25th Dec 1784	Total Interest due on 25th Dec 1784
	Brought forward	£4022 13 10	167	...	226 19 4	3855 13 10	2184 12 ..
1774 May 1st	Evert F Brown	100		...	28	100	46 11 ..
1774 April 7	Abraham c[um] Thos Rich	176 4 10½		...	36 16 8	176 4 10½	93 6 4
1774 May 1st	Joseph Paulding	235 7 ..		...		235 7 ..	175 9 ..
1774 May 19	Joseph Paulding	150		...		150	80 3 4
1774 May 28	Lewis Knistin	100		...	21	100	53 0 9
1774 May 10	John Hammond	100		...	14	100	60 7 7
1773 Dec 25	Abraham Rattan	50		...		50	38 10 3
1773 May 1st	John Junr Oakley	50		...	10 10 ..	50	30 5 6
1773 Octor 19	Thomas Buys	100		...	21	100	57 8 ..
1773 Jany 1st	Jacob Van Wert	70		...	9 16 ..	70	49 9 9
1773 June 26	James Horton c[um] Jas Horton Junr Esqre	163 2 6		...	43 12 4	163 2 6	88 1 7

Date	Name			1779 June 24		
1772 May 14th	Sam.l Deane & Zeph.l Budse.l	250	12 10 ..	140	237 10 ..	90 18 2
1773 Dec 25	Jacob Van Tessel	50	.. .. ..	10 10 ..	50	27 19 1
1772 Apl 21st	Lewis [Knistin]	80	.. .. ..	28	80	71 2 9
1773 May 8	John Morrin	100	.. .. ..	.. .. ..	100	81 8 6
1772 May 18th	Scott Esq.re John Martin Arnold	50	.. .. ..	10 10 ..	50	33 12 2
1772 Apl 25th	Hunt	100	.. .. ..	28	100	60 13 1
1772 May 27	Joseph Youngs	50	.. .. ..	14	50	30 .. 3
1772 Apl 14	Ariel Buys c[um] Ab.m Buys	200	.. .. ..	20	200	158 15 ..
1771 Dec. 25	Ezekiel and Elijah Legget	50	.. .. ..	17 10 ..	50	27 19 11
1774 June 14	Tho.s Farrington c[um] Jonath.n Fowler	100	.. .. ..	35	100	58 14 ..
	Carried forward	£6347 8 2½	179 10	715 4 4	6167 18 2½	3597 12 11

[end of ledger page]

[new ledger page]

When payable	By whom executed	Principal	Principal received	When received	Interest received	Total Principal due on 25th Dec 1784	Total Interest due on 25th Dec 1784 [3]
	Brought forward	£6347 8 2¾	179 10 ..	..	715 4 ..	6167 18 2¾	2597 12 11
1770 Mar 16	Captain James Holmes	150	..	..	73 10 ..	150	82 10 6
1770 Mar 16	Jasper Shymets c[um] John Brown	155	..		54 5 ..	155	104 14 2
1770 Feb 13	John & James Hammond	100	..		49	100	55 .. 9
1770 Nov 12	Joshua Hatfield	120	..		8 8 ..	120	110 3 7
1772 May 2d	Joshua Hatfield	100	..		..	100	88 10 9
1770 May 1st	William Lounsberry c[um] R. Bloomer	105	..		21 1 ..	105	75 12 8
1770 Sep 26	Isaac Willet Esquire	203 13 9	..		35	203 13 9	168 .. 6
1770 May 1st	Joshua Barns	120	..		42	120	81 1 6

1772 Mar 4	Adam Gilchrist	275	: : : :	: : : :	275	246 11 7
1770 Apl 29	Isaac Reade	86 12 8	: : : :	30 3 5	86 12 8	58 12 2
1770 May 1st	William Hunt	66 13 4	: : : :	9 6 8	66 13 4	59 2 1
1770 Dec 25	Jeremiah Shivers	65	: : : :	18 4 ..	65	46 10 ..
1769 May 1st	Elnathan Taylor	35	: : : :	14 14 ..	35	27 12 ..
1769 May 15th	Israel Honeywell Junr	100	: : : :	49	100	60 5 4
1769 July 14	Lieut Willm Brown	300	: : : :	147	300	177 7 3
1769 Apl 6th	Saml Purdy c[um] S. Purdy Junr	100	: : : :	49	100	60 19 5
1769 Feby 11	John Van Cortlandt	300	258 .. .. 1776 May 11	173 5 ..	42	26 17 8
1768 Dec 17	Absolom Gidney	100	: : : :	56	100	56 3 1
1767 Dec 24	Soloman Purdy	100	: : : :	56	100	63 0 5
	Carried forward	£8929 7 11½	437 10 ..	1602 1 5	8491 17 11½	5246 8 2

[end of ledger page]

[new ledger page]

When payable	By whom executed	Principal	Principal received	When received	Interest received	Total Principal due on 25th Dec 1784	Total Interest due on 25th Dec 1784
	Brought forward	£8929 7 11½	437 10 ..	....	1602 1 5	8491 17 11½	5246 8 2
1776 Apl 1st	John Hadley (read George Hadley)	200	......	....	126	200	136 5 10
1765 Dec 25	Peter Van Texels	75	.....	....	52 10 ..	75	89 5 ..
1765 Jany 20	William Pugsley	80	.....	....	61 16 ..	80	49 14 10
1765 May 10	Joshua Sherwood	80	.....	....	61 12 ..	80	48 6 1
1765 Aug 20	Anthony Fowler	50	.....	....	13 13 6	50	53 0 10
1764 May 3d	John Dusenberry	100	.....	....	77	100	67 10 4
1763 July 1st	John Miller & Stephen Holmes	52	.....	....	38 10 ..	52	39 4 10
1763 Mar 15	Caleb Archer	120	.....	....	110 4 ..	120	71 19 6

1775 May 1st	Note Caleb Artsea	40	20		20	16 12 2
1776 Dec 25	Note Talman Pugsley	40			40	22 8 ..
1776 Apl 12	Note William Haight	45 18 ..		22 1 ..	45 18 ..	87 1 6
1774 Dec 25	Dᵒ John Martine	20			20	14 .. ..
1774 Dec 25	Dᵒ John Oakley	25			25	15 15 2
1774 Dec 25	Dᵒ William Fisher	6			6	4 4 ..
1771 Apl 12	Bond Philip French	237 18 6			237 18 6	228 2 11
1775 Dec 25	Note John Stonn	35			35	22 .. ..
	Total Currency	£10136 4 5½	457 10 ..	2165 7 11	9678 14 5½	6211 19 2
	Total Amount in Sterling Money	£ 5703 12 6	257 7 ..	1218 0 6	5444 6 0	3494 4 5

(1775 Apl 5)

[end of ledger]

A List or Particular of Personal Property Taken
From Frederick Philips, Esquire by the American Army,
Being the Particular (Letter A) Referred to.

	New York Currency	Sterling Money
20 Horses at £12 each	240: –:–	
133 sheep at £1:10 each	199:10:–	
4 large stall fed oxen at £50 each	200: –:–	
40 hogs at £5 each	200: –:–	
Wagons, carts and farming utensils	80: –:–	
14 milch cows at £7 each	100: –:–	
13 young cattle at £3 each	39: –:–	
4 oxen at £10 each	40: –:–	
4 pipes of old Madeira wine at £80 each	320: –:–	
3 young Negroes at £70 each	210: –:–	
New Petteauger	30: –:–	
2 mules at £20 each	40: –:–	
	1,698:10:–	
Total Amount in Sterling Money		£955:8:–

Oct. 25, 1784

Evidence on the foregoing memorial
of *Frederick Philips*, Esquire.

Claimant Sworn

Is a native of America, born in New York. At the
commencement of the troubles in 1775, he was settled on his
manor of Philipsburgh, where he had resided for upwards of
30 years. On the appearance of the troubles, he joined a body
of loyal subjects, who associated together for the purpose of
maintaining and supporting legal government. This was in
the Spring of 1776. There was a large party raised against
them who, assisted by the New England forces, got the
better of them. The claimant, on the 6th of August, was taken
prisoner and carried into New England, where he was de-
tained 6 months, but not made close prisoner. He had afterwards a parole given him, with leave to go to New York,
where he remained during the whole war. He came into
England from thence, immediately before the evacuation
and arrived here in December 1783. He is banished and his
estate confiscated by an act of the State of New York, passed
the 29th of November, 1779. He had five sons in the British
service during the War, two of whom died, and for whom he
had purchased commissions, and is now indebted for the
money and for the purchase of those commissions.

He has never signed any association, taken any oath, or
made any concessions to the Americans during the course of
the war.

He was 25 years a member of the general assembly at
New York, and in 1775 used all his influence therein to reject
the proposition for subjecting the people to the authority of
the Congress, which at that time was successful.

Was formerly Colonel of the militia of West Chester
County and has had no commission for many years.

He had an allowance of £200 a year at New York from the
time of his coming in and he continues to receive a like
allowance from the treasury.

Certificate from General Robertson, Dated 26th October, 1783, to Loyalty, Respectability, and Exertion.

For title to his landed estate he produces.

The original grant from King William and Queen Mary,
dated 1693, June 12, whereby the tract of land granted is
erected into a manor or lordship by the name of the manor of
Phillipsborough, with power of holding a court leet and court
baron and all other powers usually attending thereon.

Real
property
for life

The will of Frederick Philipse, Esquire, of New York, his late father, deceased, dated 6th June, 1751, whereby after reciting that his Uncles, Adolph Philipse and Jacobus Van Cortland, formerly purchased of John Richbell, a certain tract or parcel of land situated at Mamaroneck, in the County of West Chester, and afterwards his said Uncle, Jacobus Van Cortlandt, for a valuable consideration, conveyed all his estate in said land to said Adolph Philipse, his heirs and assigns, which by his death was come to testator as his heir-at-law, he gives and devises the same (inter alia) to his eldest son, Frederick Philipse, and to his heirs and assigns, except so much thereof as might interfere with or run over brooks river, into the Manor of Philipsborough, all which part thereof which might so interfere, it was his will should remain and be deemed and taken as part of the said Manor of Philipsborough.

As to all the several tracts and parcels of lands and meadows, bridge toll fees, houses and lots of ground following, all the said Manor of Philipsborough as the same was then in his possession, and all those tracts and parcels of land in West Chester County that are on the East side of Hudson's River, and are bounded to the northward by a creek or river commonly called by the Indians, Kicktawank, and by the English, Knoteus, or Kroteus, River, and so eastward into the woods along the said creek or river, two English miles, and from thence upon a direct just line to Bronk's River, and so running southward along the said Bronk's River, as it runs, until a direct west line cutteth the south side of a neck or island of land, at a creek or kill called, Panarinimo, which divides York Island from the main, and so along the said creek, or kill, as it runs to Hudson's River, and continues, dividing the said York Island from the main, and so from thence to the northwards along said Hudson's River until it comes into the aforesaid creek or river called by the Indians Ricktaurank, and by the English, Knoteus, or Kroteus River (except the farm in the possession of William Jones, thereafter devised). Also the bridge called King's Bridge, and all the fees, perquisites and tolls thereto belonging. Also all his meadows situated and being in Orange County, joining upon Hudson's River between the said river and the mainland. And also a certain house and lot of ground then late in the tenure or occupation of the widow Carre. And then in the possession of William Hammersley. And certain lot of ground facing Duke Street in the rear of the said house and lot of ground where John Pintaret then lately lived and were then in the possession of said William Hammersley or his son. And also all that dwelling house, store house, and lot of ground situated in Stone Street in the City of New York then in possession of his son-in-law, Beverley Robinson. He devised and bequeathed the same (subject to the annuity thereafter mentioned) in manner following, viz.

To the use of his eldest son, Frederick Philips, for life without impeachment of waste, remainder.

To the first and other sons of his eldest son, Frederick entail, male, in strict settlement, remainder.

To his son, Philip, for life, without impeachment of waste, remainder.

To his grandson, Adolph, son of his son, Philip, for life without impeachment of waste, remainder.

To the first and other sons of said Adolph, entail, male, remainder.

To the younger sons of said Philip, according to seniority, entail male, remainder.

To such other sons as should be begotten by the testator, entail, male, to take in seniority, remainder.

To his three daughters, Susannah, Margaret and Mary, and their heirs and assigns forever, to be equally divided between them.

He charges the said Manor of Philipsborough with an annuity of £400, New York currency, to be paid to his wife, Joanna.

He devises to his said son, Frederick Philips, and his heirs, his corner house, fronting the Broadway and Stone Street, with a lot of ground and the house and ground where John Roome, then lived and his storehouse and lot of ground fronting New Street, and the two houses fronting the Broad Street, adjoining to the said lot of ground.

The said will is duly executed according to law in the presence of three witnesses.

By a codicil to the said will dated 22nd July, 1751, inter alia, he increases the annuity given to his wife to £500, New York currency, per annum.

As to the Manor of Philipbro, part of the estates devised by the aforesaid will.

Mrs. Joanna Philipse, his mother, to whom the annuity is given by the aforesaid will and codicil, and charged upon the said estate, is since deceased. Says the extent of the Manor of Philipsborough was about 24 miles in length upon Hudson's River, and about 5 miles in depth back from the river.

Says the rent roll annexed to the schedule to the best of his belief is justly stated whereby the rents of this estate and of two houses in New York which are rented at £100 currency a year, each appear to have amounted to £1,588:15 sterling, per annum, including 500[1] a year currency, which he received by way of fines or transfers of leases from one tenant to another. This had been the state of his rent roll for near 20 years, his estate not having improved owing to his having agreed with his tenants not to raise their rents for a certain number of years, but he had it in agitation to have raised the rents about the time of the troubles commencing. The rents were very regularly paid him every year. They were rather acknowledgements than rents. He should have doubled the rents with great ease. Every part of the estate was let, except his own domain, which consisted of about 3,000 acres.

He claims for his life interest in this estate and also for the rents thereof from 26th December, 1776 to 25th December, 1784, excepting some few which were received. The rents amount to £12,710 sterling.

He says he is unable to fix a value upon the estate, but he is of opinion the whole of his land and property is worth much above £100,000, sterling.

The mansion house and domain.

Says his mansion house, stables and outbuildings cost him between £7 and £8,000 currency. He had besides grist mills, with three pair of stones, besides saw mills. The domain about the mansion house was 3000 acres upon the produce of which he maintained a large family of about 50 persons. Great part of the tract was in woodland. This estate was worth £600 currency, per annum, including the income of the mills, and he claims (besides the value of his life estate) for the rent of this for the same time as the former.

Every part of the manor is under improvement.

As to 100 acres of salt meadow in Orange County:

This is also comprised in the devise entail in the will of his father.

The rent of this, he says, was worth £100 of currency per annum and the fee simple, £20, currency per acre. Claims for his life interest in this and the rent for the same time as the former.

As to a house and land at King's Bridge:

He derives his title to this house which he says has 70 acres of land to it under the aforesaid will, by which he is entitled to the life interest in this estate.

This stands just at the point of New York Island. He rented it for £100 currency a year.

The house was built by his father cost altogether £1,300 pounds currency. Values the fee simple at £2,000 currency.

Claims for his life interest and the rent for the time passed from December 1776. Two houses on Dock Street:

These are devised to the claimant for life by the aforesaid will. They would have let before the troubles for £50 currency a year.

Can't set a value on them, but thinks they were worth
£2,000 currency.

A store and lot in Stone Street.

Let this before the war to Mr. Colden for £100 currency
per annum. The house and store was burned in the first fire at
New York.

Can't value the lot on which the house stood, but thinks
it was worth £700 currency.

**Real
Estate
in fee**

As to a lot of land situated at the corner of Stone Street,
New York. This is devised to the claimant in fee by the
aforesaid will. There had been a house, but it was pulled
down about 12 years ago, he has made nothing of it since.
Worth between 7 & 800^l currency. Was offered 700^l currency for it, but did not think it price enough.

As to a lot of land in New Street, New York.

This is devised to the claimant in fee by the aforesaid
will, values it at £300 currency. He had built a coach house
and stables on it during the troubles.

As to a tract of land called "Richbell's Neck".

This is devised to him in fee by the aforesaid will. He
omitted to put it in his memorial, being ill at the time
his schedule was drawn out. The tract was purchased by his
ancestor, Colonel Richbell, for 1,000^l. He had never derived
any advantage from it, as many people had set down upon it,
and he could not drive them off without a lawsuit, which he
did not think it worth the expense of it. Only one tenant of
200 acres, Dr. Bailey, owned him as landlord. He did not
bring a suit before the troubles, as it would have been very
expensive and very uncertain.

**Personal
Estate**

He had 3 Negroes, which he valued at £70 currency
each.

20 horses, some work, some saddle. Was offered £45
currency for one a few days before they were carried off.

133 sheep at £1:10, currency each.

4 large stall-fed oxen. Had been kept up 2 years. Values
them at £50 currency each.

40 fat hogs at £5 each currency.

Wagons, carts and farming utensils, £80 currency.

14 milch cows. £7 each currency.

30 young cattle, £3 each currency.

4 pipes of old Madeira wine at £80 currency each.

A Petteauger. £30 currency cost that.

2 mules. £20 currency each.

All the foregoing things were taken off his estate by the

Rebels except the mules, which were taken by the British, the 16th Dragoons.

The amount of bonds and notes due to him with the interest thereon is £15,890:13:7-½ Currency.

He supposes that all these will be paid into the state, if they are not already (except the debt from one Billings, which he understands has been paid to his agent) as his personal as well as real estate is confiscate.

There was not mortgage or incumbrance on his estate; he owed nothing in America before the war, and the trifle he does owe has been contracted during the war.

Colonel Beverley Robinson, Sworn.

Has known the claimant for many years and particularly about the time of the breaking out of the troubles. His conduct was perfectly loyal.

Manor of Philips-borough   He has a general knowledge of the Manor of Phillipsborough which was esteemed to be 24 miles in length on the North River. There was no disputed property.

On a part of it at the northernmost end there was a piece about which there had formerly been a dispute with the Manor of Cortland, but he does not include that in what he speaks of. He cannot tell the precise number of acres. His own demesne was between 2 and 3,000 acres. Should suppose his rents from this estate must have been between £2,500 and £3,000, currency per annum, over and above the other advantages attending it, but he never saw the rent roll.

He always understood the eastern part to have been the most valuable in point of soil, but the other side next to the river was more convenient for water carriage to New York. Says that the custom upon which the tenants held their farms from the claimant was when the tenants were changed, they sold the value of their improvements and paid the landowner a 3rd of the improvement for the 1st sale, and a 6th for every sale afterwards.

Says when Colonel Phillips came to the estate, he more than doubled the rents, and he thinks on that occasion he promised not to raise them again during his life, but that his son when he should have arrived at the possession of it might have doubled or trebeled the rents.

Says he cannot pretend to say whether the claimant could have turned out any of his tenants at his own will, because there never having been any dispute it never became a question.

He has no doubt if he had been possessed of the fee simple of the estate instead of the life interest only, he could have sold it and turned out all the tenants if he chose so to do.

The mansion house was an exceeding good one and he had 2 sets of mills. One mill let to Mr. William Pugsley for £200 a year currency; another to Israel Underhill for £150 currency a year. He had besides a mill in his own hands.

Says if the fee simple of this estate was to have been sold, he has not a doubt it would have fetched £150,000 pounds New York currency with all the circumstances attending it.

Is asked if he had £20,000 in hard money, if he would have, have given it for this estate.

Says if he had £100,000 sterling in hard money, he would have given it for the estate. And thinks he should make a prodigious deal of money by it.

Supposing the claimant to have the absolute power over the land and with the power of removal of tenants at will without trouble, he thinks it would have been worth £450,000, or £500,000 pounds, New York currency.

Says there was not an acre of land on the estate except the domain, which was not tenanted.

Is asked again what he thinks to be the value of the estate as Colonel Phillips was circumstanced (supposing it not entailed).

Says he thinks it would have been worth what he has before mentioned; viz., £150,000 currency.

Is asked if he knows General DeLancey's property, and whether it was equal to Colonel Phillips's.

Says he is not particularly acquainted with General DeLancey's property, especially that in the Jerseys, but he conceives Colonel Phillips's property was worth infinitely more than General Delancey's. He was always esteemed a man of greater property than General Delancey.

Is asked if he thinks the land was the absolute property of the claimant.

He says he does not well know how to give a regular answer to the question. In some sense it might be said not to be, and yet he certainly must look upon him as the proprietor. He could not turn off a tenant because he did not like his face, but he had at the same time the power of raising their rents which was tantamount to it. If a tenant died, the son could not remain without license from the landlord. And if a tenant wished to sell his improvements, he was under the necessity of obtaining leave of the landlord before he could do it.

He is shown the rental. He says he believes it to be a just statement of the rents, but not knowing the rents of his own knowledge, he can only speak as to his belief.

He is asked what he thinks would be the value of the farm by way of annual rent. Says he thinks it was worth to a farmer £350 or £400 a year, who would make money by it. It was worth more to Colonel Phillipse.

Salt
Meadow

Knows the salt meadow in Orange County. Includes this in the valuation he has made of the estate.

Thinks it is worth 30^s currency an acre annually by way of rent. If it was to be sold in small parcels it would sell for 30 or £40 currency an acre.

Dock
Street
Stone
Street

Knew two houses the claimant had in Dock Street, New York. They were worth £1200 currency.

Knew a lot he had in Stone Street on which there was a house which was burned down. It was worth £300 currency to have built again upon, including a store which was not burned.

Knew the corner lot in Stone Street, where a house had fallen or been pulled down. Values it at £300 currency.

New
Street

Knew he had a lot in New Street, but can't speak to the value of it.

The claimant had good sheep. Should not value them at 30 [shillings]. Values them at 8 [shillings] a head, on the average, but he might possibly be able to sell them for 14 or 15^s each, as they were better than usual.

Knew the four fat oxen, they were remarkably large. Thinks they would have sold before the war for a £100 a pair.

His hogs were very fine. Pork used to sell from 30 to 40^s per hundred weight.

Thinks his farming utensils, wagons and carts, might be worth £80 currency.

A good pipe of Madeira in 1774 would fetch £100. A new pipe about £60 currency.

Captain Frederick Phillips, sworn.

Is nephew to the claimant whom he has known from his infancy. His loyalty is unquestionable.

Knew the Manor of Philipsborough. Cannot speak to the income arising from it, but it was generally esteemed to be one of the first estates on the Continent of North America. Cannot tell the exact extent of it.

The mansion house was very good, as much so as any in the Province, and the claimant lived in an elegant style for that country.

He had good mills near his house, which were of considerable value.

Knows the claimant had a house in Stone Street, New York, in which Colonel Robinson formerly lived and was burned down.

Knew his two houses in Dock Street. Should suppose

the houses and lots worth £200 that currency. Knew a lot of land the corner of Stone Street, but not knowing the dimensions of it, cannot speak precisely to the value. It may be worth 5 or £600 that currency.

Says he can only speak in general terms that the claimant possessed a very large and valuable estate and that his loyalty was unshaken.

Says he cannot speak particularly to the income of the claimant, but as long as he can recollect, it was esteemed to be much below what from the value of the estate it ought to have been., & which arose from his lenity, to his tenants, for which he was much blamed by his friends.

December 4, 1784.
James DeLancey, Esquire, Sworn.

Was well acquainted with the claimant. His conduct was uniformly loyal. He was a member of the Provincial Assembly at New York and always voted with the party who favored the measures of government.

Has been over part of his property. It was very considerable & ran 24 Miles upon Hudson's River.

Says he remembers to have heard it said, and he believes it, that on the death of his father the claimant's rents amounted to £1,000 per Annum, and he then doubled them so that they amounted to £2,000 per annum, New York currency. Speaks of the Manor of Philipsborough.

Says he has heard that the tenants understood that some agreement had been made with the ancestors of Colonel Philips that their rents should not be raised, but that he thinks that would not be the case, as the claimant had raised their rents, and it was generally understood at New York that his son would do the same when he should come to the possession of the estate.

It was usual for the tenants to sell their improvements, and upon such sale, the landlord used to have ⅓ᵈ for his assent.

Says he himself should have thought the tenants were something in the nature of copyhold tenants, if the claimant had not raised the rents, but says it was the general opinion of the lawyers at New York that the son of the claimant could raise the rents when he came to it.

If it were a fee simple estate, he would give £100,000 sterling for it tomorrow, if he had the money, he thinks it worth a great deal more and he could get a great deal by selling it again.

Says he did not consider it as a fee simple estate. He

thought they could not be turned out, but that he could raise the rents when he pleased. He supposes there was some agreement with the tenants that their rents should not be raised again during his life.

Is asked whether the tenants had that right which they could uphold against the landlord in a court of law to prevent their being turned out.

Says he is ignorant of the law in this respect, he thinks they could not be turned out.

Knows the mansion house and the buildings about it and should suppose the house, mills and domain of 3,000 acres would let for between 3 and £400 currency. It was a place that few men would take, and would be difficult to find a tenant for it. Very few men could afford to pay that rent in that country.

King's
Bridge

Knew the tavern at Kings bridge. This was likewise entailed. With a small farm to it, it let at £100 per annum, currency. If 70 acres, should imagine the house and land to be worth £1,500 currency, to be sold, is confident it would sell for that.

Stone
Street

Knows a lot of land on the corner of Stone Street, it was vacant, the house having been pulled down. Should suppose it must be worth £500 currency, but not knowing the dimensions he can't be particular as to its value. If he knew the extent, he should value it by the foot. It is a situation that would have sold at any time.

Rickbells

Says Rickbells was called disputed lands. The claimant was in possession of one farm. His own (witnesses) family had a claim upon that patent.

Dock
Street
Stone
Street

Houses on Dock Street were very valuable, but don't know where the claimant's were.

Knew the house and lot on Stone Street where Colonel Robinson lived and afterwards Mr. Colden. It was worth £1200 currency without the buildings. With them, £2,000.

Philipsburgh

Supposing the tenants to be fixed and not removable, he should suppose the estate in that case to be worth £42,000 sterling. This is supposing it to be under all the circumstances of copyhold estate.

The claimant has more sons than one, but the eldest son only is attainted.

December 13th, 1784.
The Reverend Samuel Peters, Sworn.

Knows the estate called Philips's Manor. Says he understands Colonel Philips's ancestor granted leases to the settlers on his estate. Some forever, some for 999 years, & some for 99 years, and some for 3 lives. The tenants were to pay for a certain period a rent of an ear of corn, and afterwards a certain rent per annum. The tenants could sell their farms, but not without the approbation of the owners of the estate. There was no stipulation in the lease that he should take any particular part of the purchase money, but he always insisted on having a third of what the tenant's rights sold for. Speaks of a particular instance which came within his own knowledge of a widow who sold her husband's rights on his death. They sold for £1200, New York currency. Colonel Philips insisted on having £400. The widow thought this very hard and consulted the lawyers of Connecticut upon the occasion, but could get no redress. Says he understood it was the rights which the tenants had under their leases which were sold. The fee simple value of the land would have been £1200 sterling. The land is not in itself good land, but valuable from its situation. He has often heard that Colonel Philipse took something by way of acknowledgement upon the deaths of his tenants.

Has heard of Colonel Philipse's buying some of his tenants out. He always bought their rights cheap. They got into his debt and he would throw them immediately into jail and so get rid of them.

Says he believes that the rise of the annual rents of the estate (except the back rents) depended not upon the will of Colonel Philipse or his family, but upon fixed periods settled in the original lease. Is asked whether upon the expiration of the term of the lease the land reverts to Colonel Philipse in fee.

Says he believes it did revert absolutely to him.

Says the whole of his evidence arises from information and conjectures, except as to the affair of the widow.

The Reverend Doctor Henry Monro can give information respecting the matter. He lived at Philipsburgh many years. He and Colonel Philipse did not agree, which was the reason they parted, but he doubts not he could give true information, respecting it.

December 17, 1784.
John Watts, Esquire, Sworn.

As to Philipsburgh.

Says he knows nothing but by common report. Says that the leases were originally at will, but by degrees it became the custom for the tenants to sell their farms with the landlord's consent, the landlord taking a third of the value of the first sale; afterwards a sixth on all subsequent sales. Says they have no such thing as a copyholder's state in America, but many farms on Mr. Philips's estate seem to be tending toward a copyhold. It seemed hard that were a farm had been bought in this way with the landlord's consent that the tenant should afterwards be turned off. Says he believes a great part of the estate never having been bought and sold among the tenants was not at all tending towards copyhold. His opinion of these latter lands is that the tenants might be turned off when the landlord pleased, without injustice.

He is asked whether a tenant having a title by purchase of another with the landlord's consent, could in his opinion, plead that title in a court of law.

He says it is a question which never has been tried.

He thinks if Mr. Philips had determined upon raising his rents, the courts of law would have supported him in it, but in the cases where improvements have been sold with his consent, it would not have been thought fair by people in general of those who had never sold, he conceives he might raise the rent or turn them out whenever he pleased.

Says almost all the lands in New York have been settled originally by intruders. People were very glad that others should set down on their lands. The common custom of leases where this happened was to grant a lease originally for 7 years, afterwards for a small rent and at a certain time land reverted again positively into the hands of the original landlord.

Says he has often heard conversations among lawyers upon the subject of Mr. Philips's estate, and opinions differed as to his power of turning out tenants who had come in by purchase, but none respecting those who came in otherwise.

Says Mr. Philips and his father were always considered as very mild landlords. He never heard of his putting his tenants in prison, nor that there was anything improper in the original settlement of the estate.

He believes the whole of the estate of Colonel Philips is confiscated. He has always understood so, and that they will pay no attention to the entail.

Can't form any idea of the value of the estate. He believes it was all occupied. He never heard of any written leases.

John Tabor Kempe, Esquire.
Late Attorney General of New York,
Sworn.

As to Philipsburgh.

Says he cannot speak with precision upon the nature of Mr. Philips's property, ps's property, only from general rumour. He never heard of any dispute between Colonel Philips and his tenants, therefore, it never came to any judicial decision that he knows of.

He has understood that the forefathers of Mr. Philips permitted settlers originally to come upon these lands at small rents, as tenants at will, he never heard of any written leases.

He has understood when the present Colonel Phillips came into possession of the estate, that he raised the rents. That this caused some uneasinesss among the tenants, which caused a promise to be given that he would raise them no more during his life, but it was thought that there would be another raising on the next descent.

He has heard of tenants selling their improvements but he apprehends Colonel Philips's consent was necessary, and that without it the bargain would be void, that no tenants could be brought on the estate who he should disapprove of. Mr. Philips on sales received a part of the value of the improvements.

The promise not to raise the rents, he understood to be a mere gratuitous promise, and that the tenants expected they would be raised again by Mr. Philips's son on his coming into possession. Thinks that Mr. Philips might have raised them himself if not restrained by this promise.

Says his own private opinion was that Mr. Philips's estate was not copyhold, but that it was verging very fast towards a copyhold and in process of time would have become so.

Says where a person had come in by purchase and Mr. Philips had taken a part of the purchase money, he thinks that a court of equity would have compelled him to permit the tenant to continue on the estate or sell his improvements, as it would be understood that by taking a part of the purchase money he had virtually entered into engagement to do so. Doubts whether any such right could be set up by a tenant in any case where he had not actually received a part of the purchase money.

He understood the agreement between Mr. Philips & his tenants was that the tenant should have permission to sell the improvements he had made on the land, and in that case Mr. Philips should have the refusal, and in case he did not chose to purchase, that he should have a proportion of the value. He speaks of the improvements being sold, not the soil.

He says he is unable to form a precise opinion as to Mr. Philips's power of turning out his tenants that had not purchased.

Being asked again whether in his opinion it would have been in Mr. Philips's power to have turned out his tenants by ejectment. He says he thinks it possible and almost amounting to a probability that he would have failed in an ejectment, but every tenant's case would stand upon its own grounds. Applies this to tenants who had not come in by purchase.

Mr. Philips's idea was that he could turn out his tenants when he pleased.

Says he is persuaded that Mr. Philips's estate is absolutely confiscated and lost. He believes the act passed in New York for converting estates entail into estates in fee was aimed particularly against Colonel Philips's estate. He believes he and his family have lost the fee of the estate.

Notwithstanding what he has said of the holding of the tenants, he thinks it was in the power of the landlord to raise the rents.

Says he considers the value of this estate as being worth 5 or 6^l an acre.

They have no such thing in America as selling estates at so many years purchase.

Says he is of opinion that Mr. Philips's estate was by far the best in North America, at the breaking out of the troubles. It was the most productive of rents of any (does not include in this proprietary estates). Corrects himself and says it was the best as being the most productive.

December 21st, 1784.
Colonel Beverley Robinson, Sworn.

Salt Meadow

Desires to correct his evidence as to the Salt Meadow in Orange County, and says that when he mentioned 30^s currency per acre, he was above the value greatly. He thinks 10^s per acre nearer the value.

Oxen

As to the oxen, he thinks they should be valued only at 60 or 70^l currency per pair.

Dock Street

The valuation of the 2 houses at £1,200 is cheap, but it may stand.

The same as to the lots on Stone Street.

Philipsboro

Says neither Colonel Philips nor any of his ancestors ever granted any lease in writing to any of his tenants (except one of the upper mills). They thought they had the tenants more in their power by this means.

Belives the greater part, if not the whole of the estate of Philipsburgh, had been in the habit of being sold by the tenants with the landlord's consent.

Many of the friends of the family had persuaded Colonel Philips's father to let his lands out upon leases instead of keeping them at will, but he never would consent.

Says he himself when he came to his own estate found it in much the same state as Colonel Philips's was, but he bought out the improvements of them and put then all under lease.

Knows Colonel Philips did raise his rents considerably when he came to the estate, and he believes his son would have done the same when he should come to the estate.

Thinks Colonel Philips could have raised the rents but

for his having engaged not to do so during his life, when he came to the estate.

Says it was the opinion of the country that he might turn out the tenants by ejectment, if he had taken that mode, but it is a question which never was tried.

Says the common way of making purchases in New York was by paying a third of the money down—a third in a year—and another third in two years. The installments bearing an interest sometimes, and sometimes none. The lands commonly mortgaged for the security of the payment. Sometimes the payments were in fourths or longer periods. Ready money always would purchase lands much cheaper. In estates untenanted it would make a fourth difference in the purchase money to pay it down. Never knew a tenanted estate sold. Never knew a large tract sold except unsettled tracts on the frontiers. Much depended upon the security the vendor thought he had for his money and the price of the purchase.

The Memorial of Frederick Philips, Jr. [IV]

To the commissioners appointed by Act of Parliament

for inquiring into the losses and services

of the American Loyalists.

The memorial of Frederick Philips, Junior
Respectfully showeth

That at the commencement of the late rebellion in America, your memorialist was entitled under the last will of his grandfather to a very extensive and valuable tract of land near the City of New York, known by the name of the Manor of Philipsburgh, as tenant and remainder entail, after the death of his father.

In the year 1776, his father from principles of loyalty and attachment to the British Government, took a decided part against the measures of the seditious and was obliged to take refuge with his family, of which your memorialist was one, within the British lines at New York. And afterwards, from the same principles and motives, your memorialist was induced to enter into Your Majesty's service for the purpose of suppressing the rebellion, and is now a Captain in the regiment afoot.

That in consequence of the loyal part thus taken by your memorialist in the cause of the British Government, the rebel State of New York have passed an act of their legislature by which the person of your memorialist is attainted and the said estate confiscated to the use of the State, by which he is deprived of very valuable property derived from his ancestors & reduced from the prospect of opulence to that of poverty & distress.

Your memorialist therefore prays that you will take his case into your consideration and make such report thereon as shall enable him to obtain a compensation for his losses, sustained on account of his loyalty and attachement to the British Government.

Signed,

Frederick Philips, Junior

THE SCHEDULE AND VALUATION

OF THE ESTATE OF FREDERICK PHILIPS, ESQUIRE, JUNIOR,

CONFISCATED BY THE STATE OF NEW YORK

1. The claimant was siezed as tenant of a remainder entail
   after the death of his father of the Manor of Philipsburgh
   which yielded the annual rent of £1,588:15 sterling,
   which valued at 8 years & eleven months from purchase is   14,166: 7:1

2. Of a mansion house demesne and part of the mills where
   his father resided at, £600 sterling per annum at the same
   rate is   5,350: –:–

3. Of 100 acres of salt meadow situated in Orange County at
   £56:5:– sterling per annum at the same rate   501:11:3

   Of Kings bridge Island and house at £56:5:– ster-
   ling per annum at the same rate is   501:11:3

See the will, chart of the Manor and valuation of lives

Total in Sterling £ 20,519: 9:7

SCHEDULE AND VALUATION

Oct. 26, 1784
Evidence on the foregoing memorial of Frederick Philips, Jr. Esquire
Claimant Sworn

Is Captain upon half pay of the loyal American regiment.

Is eldest son of Colonel Philips.

Has been within the British lines during the war, and has served as an officer
since 1779, always in the Provincial troops.

He claims as remainder man entail after the death of his father in the
Manor of Philipsburgh, and the other estates settled upon him by his
grandfather's will.

Says it was the intention of himself and his father to have cut off the
entail, but previous to the troubles the claimant was not of age to join with his
father in docking the remainders, being now but 24 years of age. He thinks
his loss is greater on the whole than his father's.

He says the claim was put in for him whilst he was in America, and he is
satisfied with the mode of it as far as he understands it, but he does not
understand much about it.

Claims therefore £14,166:7:1 sterling, as the value of his reversionary
interest in the Manor of Philipsburgh.

Likewise £3,009 sterling for the value of his reversionary interest in the
mansion house and domain, valuing the same upon £600 a year currency,
instead of sterling as is stated in memorial by mistake.

Likewise, £501:11:3 sterling, for his reversionary interest in 100 acres of
salt meadow in Orange County.

Likewise, £501:11:3 sterling, for his reversionary interest in Kings
Bridge Island.

Possessed no personal property, owed no debts, nor has anything owing
to him in America.

His father is 64 or 65 years of age.

Colonel Beverley Robinson, Sworn.

Knows the claimant to be the eldest son of his father,
the elder Mr. Frederick Philips.

SECOND MEMORIAL OF FREDERICK PHILIPS, JR. (IV).

To the commissioners appointed by Act of Parliament for inquiring into the losses and services of American Loyalists.

The memorial of Frederick Philipse, Jr., respectfully showeth

That your memorialist by his late memorial exhibited to your board, set forth that he was entitled to a very extensive and valuable tract of land near the City of New York, known by the name of the Manor of Philipsburgh, with other real estates in the late Province of New York, as tenant in remainder entail, after the death of his father, and that conceiving the State of New York had only confiscated his particular interest as tenant entail, he was induced in the schedule to estimate his loss in the premises only as that of a life.

But that since exhibiting the said memorial he has discovered and finds to be true that the State of New York has by an act of its legislature passed the 12th day of April 1782, declared "that in all cases wherein any person or persons would, if this Act had not been made, have been siezed in the tail of any lands, tenements or heridatements, such person or persons shall in future be deemed to be siezed in fee simple. And further, that where any lands, tenements or hereditaments, shall heretofore have been devised, granted, or otherwise conveyed by a tenant entail, and the person to whom such devise, grant, or other conveyance shall have been made, his or her heirs or assigns shall from the time such devise took effect, or from the time such grant or other conveyance was made to the day of the passing of this Act, have been in the uninterrupted possession of such lands, tenements or heridatements, and claiming and holding the same under devise, grant or other conveyance, then such grant, devise, or other conveyance shall be deemed as good, legal and effectual, to all intents as if such tenant entail had at the time of the making such devise, grant or other conveyance, been siezed of such lands, tenements and hereditaments, in fee simple, any law to the contrary hereof notwithstanding."

That under and by virtue of this law, and the act by which the person of your memorialist was attainted, the said State of New York have siezed upon not only the right of your memorialist in the said tracts of land, but the interest of all others who might be entitled to take after him under the will of his grandfather, and have advertised the same to be sold in fee simple for the use of the State.

Your memorialist therefore prays that you would be pleased to receive a new estimate hereunto annexed of the value of the interests thus lost in consequence of his loyalty, and take again into your consideration his claim and make such report thereon as shall enable him to obtain a just compensation for the losses sustained on account of his loyalty and attachment to the British Government.

Signed,

Frederick Philips, Junior

A SCHEDULE OF THE VALUATION
OF THE ESTATE OF
FREDERICK PHILIPS, JUNIOR, ESQUIRE

	Sterling
The claimant was siezed as tenant of a remainder entail after the death of his father the Manor of Philipsburgh which yielded in rents and fines per annum	1,588:15:–
Of a like estate in a mansion house and part of the mills where the claimant's father resided which yeilded per annum	337:10:–
Of 100 acres of salt meadows situated in Orange County which yielded an annual rent of	56: 5:–
And of Kings Bridge house and island, which yielded per annum	56: 5:–
Total Annual Rent	£2,037:18:–

The Manor of Philipsburgh is 24 miles long & upon an average 6 miles broad, which contains 92,160 acres & which at the moderate computation of £3 New York Currency an acre amounts to £276,480 Currency

Total Sterling Value of the Estate in Fee Simple. The Claim-   155,520: –:–
ant further submits the value of the right which he had of
raising the rents of the tenants upon the decease of his father

Signed, Frederick Philips, Junior

DECISIONS
OF THE COMMISSIONERS*

Philips, Frederick   9th April, 1784

Mr. Smith, who married his daughter, appears for him (Mr. Philips being ill). At the commencement of the troubles he was representative of the County of West Chester, as a magistrate, etc. He endeavored to suppress the troubles & was taken prisoner in endeavoring to do his duty & was confined 16 months. He was let out on parole which he broke & came within the British lines. Upon the evacuation of New York & upon a fresh proclamation being issued against him, against his person & property he came to this country. He knows the whole of his property, has been over it all, his land and property produced to him about £1500 a year sterling. It has been confiscated, but not sold, besides a considerable sum in bonds, above £9000 sterling.

Mr. Philips has a wife & 4 daughters & 3 sons. 2 sons are on service in America. The daughters & one son are with him here & to be supported by him. He brought nothing over with him & does not believe he has now £100. Mr. Smith says that Mr. Philips had an allowance of £200 a year from Sir Guy Carlton—he is 64 years of age.

Decision. £200 per annum, from 5th Apr., 1784.

There is a certificate signed by Lord Carlisle, Governor Johnson, Mr. Eden, Governor Tryon & Governor Robertson, to the loyalty & property of Mr. Philips, & that he lost all by his loyalty.

Therefore, no further certificates or attendance required.

There are in this case all those requisites which entitle Mr. Philips to protection & bounty of government. He made great and early exertions to support the authority of this country. He has sustained immense losses and suffered great persecution. There is only one thing for which we cannot commend him. He broke his parole which was the occasion (& perhaps the just occasion) of his being proscribed, but when we consider that he did all that to serve this country, perhaps it is an additional reason to give him a comfortable support.

He is besides an old man with a large family. Under all these circumstances we think him a very proper object of the bounty of government. We

* Examinations and Decisions on Fresh Claims for Temporary Support. December 1782 to 1790. Transcribed for the New York Public Library (1898). Book iii of Examinations and Decisions and Volume 6 of Transcript of the Manuscript Books and Papers of the Commission of Enquiry. . . .

have another reason for thinking that he deserves it because we find that Sir Guy Carleton whose constant endeavors to save the money of the public are well known to all who know him, thought it proper to give him an allowance of £200 a year at New York.

We shall make that the measure of our allowance, & accordingly recommend the same allowance (£200 a year) to be given to him here, to commence from the 5th of April, 1784.

Phillips, Frederick, Junior   Late of New York

14th June 1784.

Born in America, an elder son of Colonel Phillips who took a decided part in favor of Great Britain. Says that from principles of loyalty he also took part with Great Britain in 1779, and is now a Captain in the Army on half-pay. He is not at present entitled to any property but upon the death of his father will be entitled to the whole. He refers to his father's schedule of losses which were very considerable and for which see the case page. 215 [150]. He is a single man & lives with his father. There are no certificates nor are any necessary.

Decision.

This young man is the son of a man who has infinite merit with this country, & has sustained immense losses in its defense, therefore he comes before us with every prejudice in his favor because he appears to have followed his father's steps.

We have already recommended an allowance of £200 a year to his father who very highly deserves it. And we think we act consistently with the opinion we have of the merit of the family in saying that this gentleman ought to have no allowance.

If he had wanted support we should have given it to him with pleasure and as he admits that he has the half pay of a Captain & that he lives with his father, he admits enough for us to say that he is not in want of anything more and of course that he ought not to have any allowance.

Philips, Mrs., The Widow of Colonel Frederick Philips.

28th May, 1785

Joseph Galloway, Esquire, appears and informs us that Colonel Frederick Phillips died the 30th of last month. Before he died he had made an application for an augmentation to his allowance, but as it did not come to us in the regular way from the Lords of the Treasury, we thought ourselves not at liberty to consider it. When he died it came regularly before us as the case of the representative of a person who had an allowance.

She is the widow of Colonel Phillips and is stated to be in great distress with a large family.

£200 a year to be continued from the time of her husband's death. Decision.

We have in this instance been induced to depart from a rule which we had hitherto uniformly observed, which is to lessen the allowance to the representatives after the death of the person to whom it was originally given. But where a strict adherance to rules will lead us to injustice, we think ourselves at liberty to depart from them in a single instance for there cannot or ought not to be any rule without an exception. Upon hearing Colonel Phillips's case under the Act of Parliament and finding that he had a very extensive property in America, we thought that we had not been so liberal in our allowance to him as we had in many other cases. And if the Lords of Treasury had sent this case to us to be reconsidered, we meant to have added something to it. That opportunity being gone, we have only to consider what ought to be given to the Widow and family.

Under all the circumstances of this case, we think ourselves perfectly justified in recommending the whole of this allowance to be continued to Mrs. Phillips.

A disgruntled former Philipsburg Manor tenant complains to the Commissioners about Frederick Philipse's "inflated" claims.[1]

To The Hon. The Commissioners for American Loyalists,
Cock-pitt, White Hall

New York- Jan. 2, 1784

Gentlemen,

As many of the pretended Loyalists from America have greatly Imposed on you by false representations of their Losses, I have thought it necessary to mention one in particular; I mean Frederick phillips of this place, who on all occasions & to your board Sets forth that his Losses by Confiscation are Three or four Hundred Thousand pounds.

I have lived in this city the last 20 Years of my Life, am well acquainted with his mannor of philipsborough. It is a Tract of about 16 miles Long & Six miles broad. it was Granted in the Time of Charles or James 2^d, for Less than Ten pounds, & paying 2 buckskins a year quit Rent. Great part of it is dreadful mountains, the part capable of Improvement, he has granted to Tenants 180 acres in a farm at 20 bushels Wheat per annum Rent. there are 150 of these farms, his rent Role being 3000 bushel Wheat. at 5/o bushel is £750 Currency, which is equal to £400 Sterling a year, & that is his whole Revenue. which at 20 years purchase is worth £8000. the fee Simple.—but this madman calls it worth Three hundred thousand pounds.—Mr. Penn not above 40 Years Since offer^d in London the property of all pensilvania to Mr. Joshua Gee for Six thousand pounds, a Country as big as Ireland.

But Frederick phillipse says it is right to ask enough from the Crown having Room for abatement. I have within this 14 Years Lived on that mannor, and affirm that he never made above £400 Sterl p annum of it.—it is therefor Thog^t proper to Say this much to you, in order that the oppress^d public of my native Country may not be Imposed on by Imposters and Leeches from America.

I have the honour to be-

Gent^m
Y^r most Obedient Servt-
H. Lewis

1. Audit Office Series 13 Volume 116, Public Record Office, London.

The Loyalist Claims commissioners authorized the collection
of supportive documentary material in the United States by a
clerk, John Anstey. He was extremely diligent in his pursuits
and filed the following report in 1786 concerning the claims of
the Philipse family members.[1]

In the Case of Frederick Philipse Esquire, in respect of his Property,
called the Manor of Philipsburgh, situated in the County of West Chester, in
the Southern District of the State of New York.

The papers upon this Case are the following.
A Schedule of the gross Amount of the Sale, annexed to that of James
Delancey's Esquire, from the Commissioners of Forfeiture for the Southern
District.
A Certificate negative of Incumbrances from the Clerk of the Mayor's
Court.
D° of Incumbrances from the Secretary of the State.
D° relative to Debts from the Treasurer of the State.

to all which I beg leave to annex the following Observations.

The four Allotments first described in the Schedule to have been sold in
April 1784, were sold as appears for what was equivalent to Gold and Silver,
that is to say, for military Certificates upon Locations and Appraisements,
with a view to the value before the War, pursuant to the Direction of the Act
for that purpose, explained in my paper of general Information under the
Head of Sale, to which and to the Act in Question I beg leave to refer the
Board, but altho the Directions of the Act are express, and the Mode of
Appraisement therein prescribed, ostensibly fair, it is my Duty to mention
what has been suggested to me from many Quarters, and at the same Time to
caution the Board against receiving the same, as unquestionable Information. It has been suggested to me, that the whole of this Negotiation of
military Certificates was a Job.- None but the military were to be advantaged
by it, and some of them were Commissioners of Forfeiture at the Time- Mr.
Stoutenburgh himself has the Rank of Colonel, and his Colleague in Commission, the Peace Grade Title of General—This Observation however is not
pointed at these Gentlemen, or particularly at Mr. Philipse's Estate, because
the two Gentlemen now in Commission for this District, are both of them,
Men of reputed Honor and Integrity, and uncommonly so esteemed with
respect to their Office as Commissioners of Forfeiture, but where the Observation applies at all, it goes the length of imputing to the Commissioners the
Charge of purchasing the Land themselves, and by that means uniting in

1. For a brief discussion of John Anstey's efforts see: Mary Beth Norton, *The
   British Americans: The Loyalist Exiles in England 1774–1789* (Boston,
   1972), pp. 211–12. Documents are found in: Audit Office Series 12
   Volume 88, Public Record Office, London.

their own persons, the Capacities of a purchaser under the Act, and a Commissioner of Forfeiture, of Course the property was liable to be under valued, and bought in by the Commissioners themselves for less than one half of the bona fide value. This Fact is material to be observed in this Place, because the four Lots above mentioned, purport in the Schedule to have been sold upon Appraisements, and the observation set against the Sum Total professes, that, that Sum Total is the actual value by Appraisement, and I must confess, I cannot find, that the persons whose names appear on the Schedule as purchasers of that property, purchased the same In trust to the Use of the Commissioners. If I hear any particular Instance upon undoubted Authority, it will be my Duty to point it out, because an Appraisement in such Case tho made as the Act directs, with a view to the value before the War, being collusive, it must not be taken as a Criterion of the bona fide value at that Time.

Had the Schedule of Philipse's Estate been exemplified according to the Lots made for the Benefit of the Sale, and the Number of Farms upon the Estate, it would have been exceedingly expensive.

I imagine enough is here shown to prove that the price per Acre, could not be ascertained in any other way than by the Average of the whole. To what is suggested as a Note by Mr. Stoutenburgh, at the Foot of the Schedule, I will add what he informed me, which may serve by way of Illustration- About 150 Farms were appraised and sold- the highest Appraisement was 3£ an Acre- this alluded to the Lots sold by military Locations- the remainder of the Estate was sold at public Vendue, part as high as 10£ an Acre.

With respect to the value before the war, all the general Observations in the Case of James Delancey will apply with equal Force, as to the Case of Frederick Philipse. There is no man better acquainted with the property than Mr. Stoutenburgh, and no man more candid and more to be relied on in this Business, he assures me that the Estate has sold under its real value for the reasons assigned in Delancey's Case, and that it was fairly worth 200000£ Currency, and yet the Estate sold for 228619£ public Securities, which last Sume exceeds the fair and bona fide valuation of Mr. Stoutenburgh in the Balance of 28619£.

The paradox may be reconciled so as to illustrate an Observation in my Letter of general Information under the Head of Value, to which I beg leave to refer the Board in considering this Case, namely, that the *true Criterion* of the value of forfeited Land, if it could be ascertained by the sale fluctuates somewhere in a Medium between the Brokerage, and the nominal value of the paper purchase Money, and this for the reasons therein assigned. The purchaser feels the public Securities to be worth only one fourth of the nominal value, the State are bound by public Faith to respect the public Securities as worth their pretended value, but are conscious of the weakness and Insecurity of that public Faith, and actually feel that the Certificate is worth less, but do not openly avow it, and therefore fall upon a kind of middle deceptive mode, by which they save Appearances as to the public Credit of the State, and redeem so much more waste paper, and that is effected by maintaining the nominal value of that paper in the eye of the public, and enhancing the nominal price of the Estate. The purchaser can bear it, and the principal Object of Confiscation is more amply satisfied in the Redemption of the public Securities, but the Board if they take either the brokeraged value of these public Securities from the Amount of Sales, or the nominal worth of the Estate as a Criterion of the value at the Market, they must be deceived.

Upon the tenure of the Manor of Philipsburgh, and the Quantity of Interest Mr. Philipse had in the Estate.

The Manor of Philipsburgh is about six miles in Length, and four in Breadth, upon the North River, and became the property of Mr. Philipse the Uncle, and first proprietor by patent in the usual way from the Crown, and the Governor and Council upon an Indian purchase. The whole was occupied, but not all cultivated, nor all settled at one Time, but by Degrees. In old Philipses Time, any person who had a mind to sit down upon the Land, was allowed so to do, upon the Condition of cultivating it, and paying what was frequently known by the Name of Tithe, which was a Rent payable not always in the Proportion of one tenth of the annual produce, but diversely with respect to some Tenants in the proportion of one half, in respect to others only of one Quarter, and some two thirds, but the Rent was indifferently, as I am informed, called Tithe.

But there was one common stipulation to which they were all equally bound, namely, to carry the Corn to the Landlord's Mill, and also that all the Timber, cut on the Estate, and sawed into plank and Joice, should be sawed at his Mill, but I am informed that in the late Landlord's Time, there was a pecuniary Commutation for these Services.

There was I understand no Fine paid on casting a Descent, but there was a Fine upon a Sale of one fifth of the purchase money, but then nothing was sold by the Terre tenant but the Improvement, and the fifth part of the value of those Improvements was in Effect, the fifth part of the purchase money.

The Rent or Tithe was payable, as an Accident to the Soil, the Fine, in respect of the Improvements, and if an Estate had no Improvements, it could sell for nothing to the Tenant.

As to the Question, where the Landlord could raise his Tenants, or not, or turn them out at will, it is not agreed- The Report generally received, is that the Lord of the Fee could do both, but that Mr. Philipse the present Claimant's Father, entered into a Compact with his Tenants not to raise them, which compact would not be binding upon his Heir, but all these Questions are moot, and no one can certainly pronounce respecting them.

But be this as it may, whether he could turn his Tenants out, or not, or raise the Rent, are Questions that cannot be determined at present, but I am credibly informed that Actions are brought, and will be tried soon in order to decide them.

Treasury Office State of New York.

It is hereby certified that there has been rece[d] into the Treasury of the State of New York, on Account of Debts due to the forfeited Estate of Frederick Philipse Esq. public Securities to the following Amount to wit:

1784
Novem[r] 11th- From Isaac Oakly on Bond-   £ 389:11:11
                From do   do-   59:12: 8
                From Joshua Hatfield do-   237: -: 7
                From Israel Honeywell, Tho. Thompkins,
                Evert Brown, & Peter Forshe Bonds-   377: 1: 6
1785
March 14th-   From Elijah Hunter-   181: 5: 0
Octob[r] 21st- From Henry Lambert &
                Solomon Sherwood B[d]-   135: -:10
                From Joseph Youngs- Bond-   57: 5: 1
        31st-   From William Haight- Bond-   56: 4: 4
        31st-   From Joshua Sherwood- Bond-   96: 8: 5
                From Arnold Hunt- Bond-   125: 3: 5
                                                                 £1714:13: 9

Amounting together to One thousand Seven hundred and fourteen pounds thirteen shillings and ninepence New York Currency. And it is further certified that no Claim against the said forfeited Estate has yet been exhibited at this Office. Witness my hand this 19th Day of May 1786.

Gerard Bancker Treas[r]

Secretary's Office
of the State of New York
June 8th, 1786

I do hereby certify that at the Request of John Anstey Esquire, I have searched the Records of the said Office, and have found no Mortgage, Conveyance or other Incumbrance whatsoever, on Record or otherwise against any part of the property, late of Frederick Philipse Esqr Senior or his Son Frederick Philipse, but now of the people of this State by their Attainder.

Given under my hand at the said office the day and year above written

Robt. Harpur, D. Secr.^{y}

I Richard Hatfield Clerk of the County of Westchester in the State of New York, do Certify that I have Carefully examined and Searched the Records of Mortgages in the said County and that I do not find Entered on Record any Mortgage against *Frederick Philipse Esquire* late of the said County of Westchester. Given under my hand this first day of June one Thousand seven Hundred and Eighty Six.

Richard Hatfield

NOTES

John Shy (page 3–13)

1. Paul H. Smith, "The American Loyalists: Notes on their Organization and Numerical Strength," *William and Mary Quarterly*, 3rd series, XXV (1968), 259–77.
2. Paul H. Smith, *Loyalists and Redcoats: A Study in British Revolutionary Policy* (Chapel Hill, 1964); William B. Willcox, *Portrait of a General: Sir Henry Clinton in the War of Independence* (New York, 1964); Piers Mackesy, *The War for America, 1775–1783* (London and Cambridge, Mass., 1964).
3. Hannah Arendt, *On Revolution* (New York, 1963), pp. 111ff., 215, et passim.
4. R. R. Palmer, *The Age of the Democratic Revolution* (Princeton, 1959–65), I, 188–90; Gordon S. Wood, "A Note on Mobs in the American Revolution," *William and Mary Quarterly*, 3rd series, XXIII (1966), 635-42.
5. Oscar Zeichner, "The Rehabilitation of Loyalists in Connecticut," *New England Quarterly*, XI (1938), 308–30. Zeichner's statement that there is no general study of Loyalists after the war is still true.
6. Richard Cobb, *The Police and the People: French Popular Protest, 1789–1820* (Oxford, 1970).
7. Alexander C. Flick, *Loyalism in New York during the American Revolution* (New York, 1901), p. 88.
8. Adrian C. Leiby, *The Revolutionary War in the Hackensack Valley* (New Brunswick, 1962), pp. 36–37.
9. Carlisle to Lady Carlisle, 21 July 1778, *Historical Manuscripts Commission*, 14th Report: *Carlisle MSS.*, V, 356–57.
10. Memorandum, 1 August 1778, Clinton Papers, William L. Clements Library, Ann Arbor, Michigan.
11. Memorandum, 24 January 1778, Clinton Papers.
12. Conversation quoted in Rawdon to Clinton, 12February 1779, Clinton Papers.
13. [Elijah Hunter], 2 April 1779, Clinton Papers. Hunter is identified as a double agent by Carl Van Doren, *Secret History of the American Revolution* (New York, 1941), pp. 237 and 300–01. On Holmes: Robert Bolton, *A History of the County of Westchester* (New York, 1848), I, 27–28.
14. New York, 1 February 1779, *Carlisle MSS.*, V, 415–16.
15. Abraham C. Cuyler to Thomas Ward, 7 June 1780, Clinton Papers. Underscoring is mine.

16. The whole story is in the Clinton Papers: Samuel Hayden to John André, 27 June 1780; Cortlandt Skinner to André, 4 July; André to Stephen Payne Adye, 11 July; minutes of a board of inquiry, 18 July; André to Beverley Robinson, 19 July.

Catherine S. Crary (pages 14–24)

1. "The suffering inhabitants of Westchester County are ravaged without restraint or remorse." *Journal of the Provincial Congress*, I, 749.
2. The Cowboys were refugee Loyalists, while the Skinners in general supported the rebels. The former, sometimes called "Refugees," were raised and commanded by Major Mansfield Bearmore who was killed in November 1780. Thereafter Colonel James DeLancey of West Farms assumed command.
3. Otto Hufeland, *Westchester County during the Revolution* (White Plains, 1926), p. 237.
4. *Ibid.*, p. 417. Allison Albee's interpretation thirty years later agrees with Hufeland: "The Patriots were governed by a framework of law and order far different than the law of wanton cruelty of the Refugees [Cowboys]." The latter were "a lawless band who masqueraded as soldiers and thrived on nocturnal attacks against the defenseless," while "the Patriot Skinners worked under arrangement with the regular Continental army command. Spoils and contraband were accounted for and disposed of in accordance with established military rules." "The Defenses of Pines Bridge," *The Westchester Historian*, 34 (1958), 93; 37 (1961), 117.
5. James H. Pickering, "The Oral Tradition of the Neutral Ground," *The Westchester Historian*, 43 (1967), 5.
6. *Ibid.*, p. 6. Robert Bolton also blames principally the Skinners, calling them "banditti . . . who . . . professed attachment to the American cause; but in reality they were more uprincipled, perfidious, and inhuman than the Cowboys themselves; for these latter exhibited some symptoms of fellow feeling for their friends, whereas the Skinners committed their depredations equally upon friends and foes." *History of the County of Westchester* (New York, 1905), I, 306.
7. Carleton Papers, Vol. 50, No. 34, New York Public Library. April 3, 1783.
8. Washington to Greene, Stamford, November 12, 1776, *The Freeman's Journal or New Hampshire Gazette*, December 3, 1776, I, No. 28. See J. Thomas Scharf, *History of Westchester County*, (Philadelphia, 1886), I, 454.
9. Interview by John McDonald, November 20, 1845. McDonald Interviews, collection of, Huguenot and Historical Association, New Rochelle, N.Y. p. 304. Selections from the interviews were published as *The McDonald Papers*, William S. Hadaway, ed., 2 parts (White Plains 1926–27).
10. *Ibid.*, p. 77.
11. December 2, 1776. Scharf, I, 455, fn. 4. Gerard Beekman Jr. wrote to his father from Peekskill, June 29, 1779: "Yesterday Coll [Samuel]

Drake [of the Westchester militia] paraded by here and down to peekskill . . . to put in force his manifesto . . . He sent one Lucius from Salem & one Burlingham with a party of six more to every house to use the inhabitants ill by cuting them & beating them with their swords. They also presented their pistols to the Breast of a woman in Neighbourhood who had Laying in but 3 or 4 days. Coll Drake also sent them to my house. . . . When they came to the door they were in Liquor & behaved with the greatest insolence immaginable threat[en]ing Life, & ordered cornelia to fill their bottles. . . . " Van Cortlandt-Van Wyck Papers, Typescript at Sleepy Hollow Restorations Library. New York Public Library.

12. "Diary of Aide to Rochambeau 1781," *Magazine of American History*, IV (1880), 303.

13. McDonald Interviews, pp. 193–94.

14. Benjamin Kepp told McDonald: "The Skinners . . . were very cruel, whipping and torturing the peaceable inhabitants to extort their money from them." McDonald Interviews, p. 657.

19515. Interview with Mrs. Daniel Edwards, McDonald Interviews, p. 112.

16. *Ibid.*, p. 693.

17. The United States has recognized guerrillas as lawful combatants since 1863, when it disseminated Francis Lieber's *Instructions . . . for United States Armies in the Field*. The Geneva Conventions of 1929 and 1949 accepted guerrillas as belligerents entitled to be treated as prisoners of war when captured, if they fulfilled four requirements: if commanded by a person responsible for his subordinates, if they wore a fixed or distinctive sign or uniform, if they carried arms openly, and if they conducted their operations in accordance with the laws and customs of war. Lieber wrote that guerrillas were part and parcel of the main army, entitled to the privileges of the law of war. *Guerrilla Parties Considered with Reference to the Laws and Usages of War.* (New York, 1862), p. 11.

18. *Loyalist Transcripts*, 18, 271–83. Moses Knapp, another captain in DeLancey's corps, also says he joined the British army in 1777 and was duly commissioned by William Tryon (November 1779) and by Sir Guy Carleton in 1783. *Ibid.*, pp. 260 ff.

19. Carleton Papers, No. 7302, New York Public Library.

20. Bolton, I, 613.

21. See Albee, "Defenses of Pines Bridge," *The Westchester Historian* (1958) p. 92.

22. William S. Hadaway, ed., *The McDonald Papers* (White Plains, 1927), Part II, 6.

23. Emerich de Vattel, *Law of Nations* (Northampton, Mass., 1805 ed.), p. 419.

24. *Ibid.*, p. 416.

25. *Ibid.*, pp. 422–23.

26. McDonald Interviews, p. 175.

27. *Ibid.*, p. 243.

28. *Ibid* ., p. 110. Mrs. Edwards, however, thought Captain Samuel Knapp "cruel and severe." She said DeLancey was "stern and savage," turned

black in a passion," "knocked down a countryman because he wore his hat in DeLancey's presence." *Ibid.*, p. 108.
29. McDonald Interviews, pp. 243–45. Allison Albee has identified the Totten in this incident as Captain Gilbert Totten, whereas it was a seventeen-year-old cousin, James Totten, a private in the Cowboys. Through this mistaken identity Albee concluded that Gilbert Totten was a man of despicable nature. *The Westchester Historian*, 36 (1960), 48; 37, (1961), 114. See McDonald Interviews. pp. 243, 968, 405, 559.
30. *Ibid.*, p. 365.
31. McDonald Interviews, p. 729.
32. Robert D. Bass, *The Swamp Fox* (New York, 1959), p. 4.

Jacob Judd (pages 25–43)

1. For an overview of Loyalism in America, see Robert M. Calhoon, *The Loyalists in Revolutionary America*, 1760–1781(New York, 1973). An excellent historiographical analysis can be found in George A. Billias' essay, "The First Un-Americans: The Loyalists in American Historiography," in Alden T. Vaughan and George A. Billias, eds., *Perspectives on Early American History: Essays in Honor of Richard B. Morris* (New York, 1973).
2. The classic examination of prerevolutionary New York politics from which all interpretations flow is Carl L. Becker's, *The History of Political Parties in the Province of New York*, 1760–1776 (Madison, Wisc., 1968). An analysis of Becker and his historical methodology is the topic of Milton M. Klein's "The Dilemma of Carl Becker," in Vaughan and Billias, eds., *Perspectives on Early American History.* For a recent discussion of New York politics, consult Bernard Mason, *The Road to Independence: The Revolutionary Movement in New York*, 1773–1777 (Lexington, Ky., 1966): also see note 22.
3. For a picture of a reluctant New York rebel, see Richard B. Morris, "The American Revolution Comes to John Jay," in Jacob Judd and Irwin H. Polishook, eds., *Aspects of Early New York Society and Politics* (Tarrytown, N. Y., 1974).
4. New York Committee, Fishkill, December 13, 1776, in Peter Force, *American Archives, Fifth Series* (Washington, 1853), III, 1205–07.
5. Timothy Dwight, *Travels in New England and New York* (New Haven, 1822), III, 442–43.
6. John Jay is quoted in Robert Bolton, *The History of the Several Towns, Manors, and of the County of Westchester From Its First Settlement to the Present Time* (New York, 1881), I, 523.
7. *The New York Gazette and the Weekly Mercury*, March 13, 1775.
8. *Ibid.*, February 27, 1775.
9. Members of the General Assembly of New York to Gen. Thomas Gage, May 5, 1775 in *New-York Historical Society Collections for the Year* 1923 (New York, 1923), pp. 291–93.
10. Memorial of Frederick Philipse in *Transcripts of the Manuscript Books*

and Papers of the Commission of Enquiry into the Losses and Services of the American Loyalist . . . Examinations in London and New York, 1783–1790, New York Public Library, Vol. 41.

11. Memorial of Frederick Philipse, November 1776, in Collections of Sleepy Hollow Restorations.

12. From the Collections of Sleepy Hollow Restorations. The letters are presented in their entirety. The original spelling and punctuation have been retained. Excerpts appeared in Catherine Crary's, *The Price of Loyalty: Tory Writings from the Revolutionary Era* (New York, 1973).

13. John C. Fitzpatrick, ed., *The Writings of George Washington* (*Washington, D.C.*, 1932), VI, 222–23.

14. Colonial Office Series 5, Volume 1108, Public Record Office, London. Microfilm Reproductions in the Library of Congress.

15. Charles J. Headly, ed., *The Public Records of the State of Connecticut, from October, 1776, to February, 1778, inclusive* (Hartford, 1894), p. 152.

16. Force, *American Archives, Fifth Series*, III, 1205–07.

17. Edward H. Tatum, Jr., ed., *The American Journal of Ambrose Serle, Secretary to Lord Howe, 1776–1778* (San Marino, Calif., 1940), p. 201.

18. John R. Brodhead, ed., *Documents Relative to the Colonial History of the State of New York; Procured in Holland, England and France* (Albany, 1857), VIII, 735.

19. *The New York Journal, and the General Advertiser*, November 29, 1779.

20. Treasury Papers, Series T1, Vol. 586, Public Record Office, London.

21. John Watts Papers, September 20, 1784, New-York Historical Society.

22. John T. Reilly, "The Confiscation and Sale of the Loyalist Estates and Its Effect Upon the Democratization of Landholding in New York State 1799–1800" (Unpublished Doctoral Dissertation, Fordham University, N.Y., 1974), pp. 160–62. This study contains a comprehensive examination of the historiography relating to the Loyalist question in New York.

23. Metchie J. E. Budka, trans. & ed., Julian U. Niemcewicz, *Under Their Vine and Fig Tree: Travels Through America in 1797–1799*, 1805 (Collections of the New Jersey Historical Society, XIV, Elizabeth, N. J., 1965), 211.

William A. Benton (pages 44–55)

1. William Nelson, *The American Tory* (Boston, 1964), p. v.

2. Henry Cruger Van Schaack, *Memoirs of the Life of Henry Van Schaack* (Chicago, 1892), p. 15.

3. Henry Cruger Van Schaack, *The Life of Peter Van Schaack* (New York, 1842), p. 9. This volume is made up almost entirely of Peter Van Schaack's diary and selected letters.

4. Peter Van Schaack to John Maunsell, May 7, 1775; *ibid.*, pp. 37–39.

5. *American Archives: Fourth Series*, Peter Force, ed., 6 vols. (Washington, 1837–1846), I, 293, 295–96.

6. Peter Van Schaack to John Vargill, February 19, 1774; Van Schaack Family Papers, Columbia University Library.
7. Peter Van Schaack to John Vargil, May 13, 1774; *ibid.*
8. Peter Van Schaack to Peter Silvester, May 21, 1774; Van Schaack, *Peter Van Schaack*, pp. 16–17.
9. Peter Van Schaack to John Maunsell, May 7, 1775; *ibid.*, pp. 37–39.
10. Peter Van Schaack to James Duane, n.d., 1774; Van Schaack Family Papers, Columbia University Library.
11. Peter Van Schaack to Henry Van Schaack, February 25, 1775; Van Schaack, *Henry Van Schaack*, pp. 36–37.
12. Peter Van Schaack to Henry Cruger, Sr., September 6, 1775; Van Schaack Family Papers, Columbia University Library. Van Schaack, *Peter Van Schaack*, p.58.
13. *Amer. Arch.*: 4, VI, 1368.
14. *Minutes of the Albany Committee of Correspondence 1775–1778*, James Sullivan, ed., 2 vols. (Albany, 1923–1925), I, 423. Van Schaack, *Peter Van Schaack*, p. 60.
15. *Albany Committee Minutes*, I, 451–452. Van Schaack, *Peter Van Schaack*, p. 479.
16. Van Schaack, *Peter Van Schaack*, p. 88.
17. Peter Van Schaack to Theodore Sedgwick, August 13, 1778; *ibid.*, p. 118.
18. Theodore Sedgwick to Aaron Burr, August 7, 1778; *ibid.*, p. 119.
19. John Jay to Peter Van Schaack, n.d.; *ibid.*, p. 99.
20. Gouverneur Morris to Peter Van Schaack, September 8, 1778; *ibid.*, pp. 130–31.
21. *Ibid.*, p. 120.
22. Peter Van Schaack to the Albany Committee of Safety, January 25, 1777; Peter Van Schaack Papers, New-York Historical Society.
23. Diary, January 1776; Van Schaack, *Peter Van Schaack*, pp. 54–56.
24. *Ibid.*
25. *Ibid.*
26. *Ibid.*, pp. 73–76, 87, 260–61.
27. Peter Van Schaack to the Albany Committee of Safety, January 25, 1777; Peter Van Schaack Papers, New-York Historical Society.
28. *Ibid.*
29. Diary, November 1779; Van Schaack, *Peter Van Schaack*, p. 244.
30. Diary, 1780; *ibid.*, p. 263.
31. Peter Van Schaack to John Jay, August 5, 1783; *ibid.*, p. 309.
32. John Jay to Peter Van Schaack, September 8, 1784; John Jay Collection, Columbia University Library.
33. John Jay to Peter Van Schaack, January 1, 1784; Emmet Collection, New York Public Library.
34. Peter Van Schaack to Jane Silvester, July 1785; Van Schaack Family Papers, Columbia University Library.
35. Peter Van Schaack to Henry Walton, June 3, 1788; Van Schaack, *Peter Van Schaack*, p. 425.
36. Paul M. Hamlin, *Legal Education in Colonial New York* (New York, 1939), p. 69.

Willard S. Randall (pages 56–73)

1. Lewis Morris to Peter Collinson, May 24, 1742, *Papers of Gov. Lewis Morris*. (New York, 1852).
2. See, for example Lawrence Henry Gipson, *The Coming of the Revolution* (New York, 1954), pp. 134–35; and Richard M. Ketchum, *The Winter Soldiers* (New York, 1973).
3. David Hawke, *The Colonial Experience* (New York, 1966), p. 479; Duane Lockard, *The New Jersey Governor* (Princeton, 1964), pp. 21–30.
4. *Documents Relating to the Colonial History of the State of New Jersey*, Frederick W. Ricord and William Nelson, eds. (Newark, 1886), hereafter *New Jersey Archives* (N.J.A.), First Series, X, 689–91.
5. *N.J.A.*, XXIV, 144.
6. Leonard Lundin, *Cockpit of the Revolution* (Princeton, 1940), pp. 48–49.
7. Edwin P. Tanner, *Dictionary of American Biography*; letter from Edward Shippen to his son, Joseph, Jan. 17, 1753, Shippen Papers, American Philosophical Society; William A. Whitehead, "Biographical Sketch of Gov. William Franklin," *Proceedings of the New Jersey Historical Society*, III (1849), p. 137; Whitehead, *Contributions to the Early History of Perth Amboy* (New York, 1856); Carl and Jessica Bridenbaugh, *Rebels and Gentlemen*, (New York, 1942), pp. 111–21, 334–39.
8. *N.J.A.*, IX, 389–91; Peter Kalm, *Travels in North America* (New York, 1937).
9. Lockard, pp. 21–30.
10. Donald L. Kemmerer, *Path to Freedom: The Struggle for Self Government in Colonial New Jersey, 1703–1776*, (Princeton, 1940), pp. 266–74.
11. Whitehead, *Early Contributions*, pp. 185–207; Alan Valentine, *Lord Stirling* (New York, 1969), pp. 101–02; Thomas Penn to James Hamilton, March 11, 1763, Thomas Penn Letterbook, Penn Papers, Historical Society of Pennsylvania.
12. Valentine, p. 102.
13. Benjamin H. Newcomb, *Franklin and Galloway* (New Haven, 1972), p. 97; letter from John Penn to Thomas Penn, Oct. 17, 1764, Penn Papers, Official Correspondence, Historical Society of Pennsylvania; *Letters from William Franklin to William Strahan*, (Philadelphia, 1911), pp. 21–23.
14. Morris Schonbach, *Radicals and Visionaries: A History of Dissent in New Jersey* (Princeton, 1964), pp. 16–17; Whitehead, *Early Contributions, p.* 188; Connolly, James C., "Quit-rents in Colonial New Jersey as a Contributing Cause for the American Revolution," P.N.J.H.S., VII (Jan., 1922), 13–21.
15. George De Cou, *Burlington-A Provincial Capitol*, (Philadelphia, 1945), pp. 80–81; 102–03; 106–07; 195.
16. Edgar J. Fisher, *The Province of New Jersey* (New York, 1911), pp. 76–79; Thomas Penn to James Hamilton, Feb. 11, 1763, P.L.B. VII; William S. Hanna, *Benjamin Franklin and Pennsylvania Politics*, (Stan-

ford, 1964), pp. 147–48; John F. Burns, *"Controversies Between Royal Governors and Their Assemblies"* (Boston, 1923); G. B. Turner, "Colonial New Jersey, 1703–63;" *P.N.J.H.S.*, LXX, No. 4, (Oct., 1952), 229–45.

17. *N.J.A.*, IX, 488–90.
18. Connolly, p. 16; Gipson, pp. 134–35.
19. Catherine Drinker Bowen, *John Adams and the American Revolution* (Boston, 1948), pp. 320–24; *N.J.A.*, X, 434–51.
20. *N.J.A.*, IX, 405–24.
21. *Ibid.*, p. 448.
22. *Ibid.*, pp. 490–91.
23. Kemmerer, p. 282f.
24. *N.J.A.*, IX, 500–01.
25. Connolly, "The Stamp Act and New Jersey Opposition to It," *P.N.J.H.S.*, (April, 1924), pp. 137–50; Kemmerer, p. 285.
26. Kemmerer, p. 283–84; *N.J.A.*, pp. 497–520.
27. Newcomb, pp. 150–51.
28. Connolly, p. 150; William H. Mariboe, *The Life of William Franklin*, unpublished doctoral dissertation, University of Pennsylvania, 1962, p. 202.
29. Fred J. Cook, *The New Jersey Colony* (New York, 1969), pp. 108–28; Lundin, pp. 48–69; Mariboe, pp. 256–57.
30. Kemmerer, pp. 299–300; Catherine Fennelly, "William Franklin of New Jersey," *William & Mary Quarterly*, 3rd series, VI (1949), pp. 361–82; Harry B. and Grace M. Weiss, *Some Legislation Affecting Rural Life in Colonial New Jersey* (Trenton, 1957).
31. Gipson, pp. 139–40; Mariboe, pp. 137–54.
32. Newcomb, pp. 330–31, 338–39; *D. A. B.*; Carl Van Doren, *Benjamin Franklin* (New York, 1941), pp. 305–10; *N.J.A.*, IX, 569–70, 574–75.
33. Mariboe, pp. 148–49.
34. William Franklin papers, Mss., N.J.H.S.
35. *N.J.A.*, X, 45–48.
36. Fisher, p. 42.
37. Kemmerer, pp. 311–15.
38. Connolly, "Quit-rents. . .", pp. 13–21; Kemmerer, pp. 287, 319–20; 323–24, 326,
39. *Ibid.*, pp. 317f, 318f.
40. *Pennsylvania Packet*, No. 119, Jan. 31, 1774; *ibid.*, No. 160, Nov. 4, 1774; Fennelly, p. 38,
41. H. H. Hill, *History of the Church in Burlington* (New York, 1886).
42. *Letters from William Franklin to William Strahan* (Philadelphia, 1911), p. 21.
43. *D.A.B.*, pp. 436–38; Andrew J. Mellick, *The Story of an Old Farm* (Somerville, N.J., 1889), pp. 306–08.
44. Lucius Q. C. Elmer, *Reminiscences of New Jersey* (New York, 1876).
45. Mariboe, p. 387.
46. Newcomb, pp. 402–05.
47. Bowen, p. 491; *N.J.A.*, X, 373–75.

48. *N.J.A.*, X, 538–41.
49. Kemmerer, pp. 327–32.
50. *N.J.A.*, X, 538–41.
51. Elias Boudinot, *Journal*, N.J.H.S., pp. 4–8.
52. *N.J.A.*, X, 689–91.
53. Kemmerer, p. 343, 339–40.
54. *N.J.A.*, X, 658.
55. Van Doren, pp. 558–62.
56. *N.J.A.*, X, 719–32.
57. "Letters of Joseph Galloway from Leading Tories in America," The *Historical Magazine*, V (1861), pp. 271, 301.
58. Mary Beth Norton, *The British-Americans, The Loyalist Exiles in England, 1774–1789* (Boston, 1972), pp. 171–73.

Esmond Wright (pages 74–94)

1. Audit Office Papers, Series 12 and 13, H.M. Public Records Office, London, England.
2. Wallace Brown, *The King's Friends: The Composition and Motives of the American Loyalist Claimants* (Providence, 1966) and *The Good Americans: Loyalists in the American Revolution* (New York, 1969).
3. Eugene R. Fingerhut, "Uses and Abuses of the American Loyalist's Claims: A Critique of Quantitative Analysis," *William and Mary Quarterly*, 3rd series, XXV, No. 2 (1968), 245–58.
4. Colonial Office Papers, Series 5, H.M. Public Records Office, London, England.
5. Paul H. Smith, "The American Loyalists: Notes on Their Organization and Numerical Strength," *William and Mary Quarterly*, 3rd series, XXV, No. 2 (1968), 259–77.
6. William H. Siebert, *Loyalists in East Florida, 1774–1785* (Deland, Fla., 1929).
7. Alexander C. Flick, *Loyalists in New York During the American Revolution*, (New York, 1901).
8. Wallace Brown, "The View at Two Hundred Years: The Loyalists of the American Revolution," *Proceedings of the American Antiquarian Society*, 80 (1970), 25–47.
9. Virginia Harrington, *The New York Merchant on the Eve of the Revolution*, (New York, 1935).
10. Robert A. East, *Business Enterprise in the American Revolutionary Era*, (New York, 1938).
11. Flick, p. 81.
12. Beatrice G. Reubens, "Pre-Emptive Rights in the Disposition of a Confiscated Estate: Philipsburg Manor, New York," *William and Mary Quarterly*, 3rd series, XXII, No. 3 (1965), 435–56.
13. Staughton Lynd, "Who Should Rule at Home? Dutchess County, New York, in the American Revolution," *William and Mary Quarterly*, 3rd series, XVII, No. 3 (1961), 330–59.

14. William A. Benton, *Whig Loyalism: An Aspect of Political Ideology in the American Revolutionary Era* (Teaneck, N.J., 1969).
15. Robert M. Calhoon, *The Loyalists in the American Revolution 1760–1781* (New York, 1973).
16. L.F.S. Upton, *The Loyal Whig: William Smith of New York and Quebec* (Toronto, 1969).
17. James Kirby Martin, *Men in Rebellion* (New Brunswick, 1973).
18. William H. Nelson, *The American Tory* (Oxford, 1961).

SUGGESTED FURTHER READINGS
ON THE AMERICAN LOYALISTS

Bailyn, Bernard. *The Ordeal of Thomas Hutchinson.* Cambridge, 1974.

Benton, William A. *Whig-Loyalism: An Aspect of Political Ideology in the American Revolutionary Era.* Rutherford, N.J., 1969.

Brown, Wallace. *The King's Friends: The Composition and Motives of the American Loyalist Claimants.* Providence, 1965.

Brown, Wallace. *The Good Americans: The Loyalists in the American Revolution.* New York, 1969.

Calhoon, Robert M. *The Loyalists in Revolutionary America, 1760–1781.* New York, 1973.

Callahan, North. *Flight From The Republic: The Tories of The American Revolution.* New York 1967.

Crary, Catherine. *The Price of Loyalty: Tory Writings From The Revolutionary Era.* New York, 1973.

East, Robert A. *Connecticut's Loyalists.* Chester, Conn., 1974.

Fingerhut, Eugene R. "Uses and Abuses of the American Loyalists' Claims," *William and Mary Quarterly*, 3rd series, xxv (April, 1968), pp. 245–258.

Flick, Alexander C. *Loyalism in New York During The American Revolution.* New York, 1901.

Leder, Lawrence H., ed. *The Colonial Legacy, Vol. I, Loyalist Historians.* New York, 1971.

Nelson, William H. *The American Tory.* Boston, 1961.

Norton, Mary Beth. *The British Americans: The Loyalist Exiles in England 1774–1789.* Boston, 1972.

Sabine, Lorenzo. *Biographical Sketches of Loyalists of The American Revolution, with an Historical Essay,* 2d ed. rev., Boston, 1864.

Smith, Paul H. *Loyalists and Redcoats: A Study in British Revolutionary Policy.* Chapel Hill, 1964.

Smith, Paul H. "The American Loyalists," *William and Mary Quarterly* 3rd Series, xxv (April, 1968) pp. 259–277.

Van Tyne, Claude. *The Loyalists in The American Revolution.* New York, 1902.

Zeichner, Oscar. *Connecticut's Years of Controversy, 1750–1776.* Chapel Hill, 1949.

CONTRIBUTORS

WILLIAM A. BENTON, author of *Whig-Loyalism: An Aspect of Political Ideology in the American Revolutionary Era*, is a former Professor of History and is one of the founders of the University Seminar on Early American History and Culture at Columbia. He is currently preparing a biography of William Samuel Johnson as part of the Connecticut Bicentennial Commission's publication series.

CATHERINE S. CRARY, until her death in March 1974, was Adjunct Professor of History at Finch College. She played an active role in collecting John Jay papers for Columbia University and in the Program for Loyalist Studies and Publications. Her book *The Price of Loyalty*, a collection of Tory writings from the Revolutionary era, won her the annual award of the American Revolution Round Table for 1973. She contributed articles to *New York History*, *The William and Mary Quarterly*, and *The Mississippi Valley Historical Review*.

WILLARD S. RANDALL is a free-lance writer, editor and historian. For ten years a Philadelphia journalist, he was a writer-editor for *The Evening & Sunday Bulletin*, which nominated him in 1969 for a Pulitzer Prize. He has published more than twenty articles on Pennsylvania and New Jersey history. He recently contributed to *The Story of America*, a Bicentennial history of the United States, has completed a text on journalism and an historical guide to Philadelphia; and, with the aid of a research grant from the American Philosophical Society, is completing a full-length biography of William Franklin as well as a volume of his collected correspondence.

JOHN SHY is Professor of History at the University of Michigan, and is actively interested in both military history and early American history, particularly the history of the American Revolution. He is the author of *Toward Lexington: The Role of the British Army in the Coming of the American Revolution*, which received the John H. Dunning Prize of the American Historical Association in 1966, and is currently completing a general history of the American Revolution.

ESMOND WRIGHT is Professor of American History and Director of the Institute of United States Studies in the University of London. He is the author of *Washington and the American Revolution*, *Benjamin Franklin and American Independence*, *Fabric of Freedom*, and other studies on the Revolutionary period.

The Editors

ROBERT A. EAST is Executive Director of the Program for Loyalist Studies and Publications. As Professor of History at the City University of New York, he teaches both at Brooklyn College and at the Graduate Center. He is the author of *Connecticut's Loyalists, Business Enterprise in the American Revolutionary Era*, and *John Quincy Adams: The Critical Years, 1785–1794*, as well as of articles for *The New England Quarterly, The Journal of Economic History*, and *New York History*.

JACOB JUDD, an editor and contributor to this volume, is a member of the faculty of Herbert H. Lehman College of the City University of New York and is the Research Coordinator for Sleepy Hollow Restorations. He is co-editor (with Irwin H. Polishook) of *Aspects of Early New York Society and Politics* and has contributed numerous articles pertaining to New York history to the *New York-Historical Society Quarterly, New York History, The Journal of Long Island History*.

INDEX

A

Adams, John, 78, 80, 81
Albany, N.Y., 74
Alexander, William (Lord Stirling), 59, 62, 69
Allen, Andrew, 54
Allen, Ethan, 24
André, John, 10
Anglican Church, 25, 64, 89
Anti-Federalists, 54
Anstey, John, 147–51
Arendt, Hannah, 3
Audit Office Records, Public Record Office, London, 95, 99, 101 ff.

B

Bass, Edward, 91
Bass, Robert D., 24
Bayard, John, 79
Bayard, Robert, 84
Becker, Carl, 92
Bedford, N.Y., 8
Benton, William A., 44–55
Bergen County, 4, 6, 7, 9
Bond, Phineas, 78
Boudinot, Elias, 69
Brant, Joseph, 83, 92

Brown, Wallace, 44, 77, 79, 81
Browne, Montforte, 79
Burlington County, 65–66
Burlington, N.J. 56, 60, 67
Burr, Aaron, 49
Butler, Colonel John, 83, 92

C

Canada, 76, 77, 86, 94
Carleton, Guy, 19, 36, 143
Carlisle, Earl of, 6–7, 8, 102
Chandler, Thomas Bradbury, 91
Chappaqua, N.Y., 19, 22
Chesterton, G.K., 74
Clinton, Governor George, New York, 31, 48, 49
Clinton, General Henry, 7, 9
Closter, N.J., 7, 9
Cobb, Richard, 4
Coke, Daniel Parker, 95
Colden, Lt. Gov. Cadwallader, New York, 63
Columbia County, 54
Commissioners of Forfeiture, New York, 147–48
Committee of Safety, New York, 30, 32–33

Sleepy Hollow Restorations gratefully acknowledges the support of the New York State American Revolution Bicentennial Commission in connection with the conference on the Loyalist Americans, from which this publication was developed.